Family and Other Business Groups in Economic Development

Harry W. Strachan
foreword by
Raymond Vernon

The Praeger Special Studies program—utilizing the most modern and efficient book production techniques and a selective worldwide distribution network—makes available to the academic, government, and business communities significant, timely research in U.S. and international economic, social, and political development.

Family and Other Business Groups in Economic Development
The Case of Nicaragua

PRAEGER SPECIAL STUDIES IN INTERNATIONAL BUSINESS, FINANCE, AND TRADE

Praeger Publishers   New York   Washington   London

Library of Congress Cataloging in Publication Data

Strachan, Harry W
    Family and other business groups in economic
development.

    (Praeger special studies in international business,
finance, and trade)
    Includes bibliographical references.
    1. Trade and professional associations—Nicaragua.
2. Trade and professional associations.   3.   Economic
development.   I. Title.
HD2429. N5S7   338. 97285   75-25025
ISBN 0-275-56050-3

PRAEGER PUBLISHERS
111 Fourth Avenue, New York, N.Y. 10003, U.S.A.

Published in the United States of America in 1976
by Praeger Publishers, Inc.

Printed in the United States of America

for Deirdre

FOREWORD
Raymond Vernon

The past two decades have generated a great tide of research on the subject of economic development. Yet some of the most provocative and distinctive phenomena that are associated with the development of poor countries have often been passed over by trained and disciplined researchers, to be left for treatment in the Sunday supplement and the casual travelogue.

One reason for this systematic neglect is obvious. The phenomena we think of as distinctive in the development process have a habit of straddling the disciplines. They rarely lend themselves to rigorous treatment solely by the economist or the political scientist or the sociologist or the specialist in management science. Accordingly, they demand an uninhibited willingness on the part of the researcher to stretch beyond the safe and familiar categories of systematic human knowledge in order to deal with his chosen subject.

Practically every developing country has generated its business groups in one form or another, and has allowed them to develop a central role in the modernizing process. Descriptions and analyses of the performance of these groups, however, are hard to find. Here and there one could find a perceptive account of one institution or another that seems to be a first cousin to the phenomenon of the business group, such as the zaibatsu in the development of Japan, the auslanders in the development of African economies, or the occupational castes and families in the Asian subcontinent. But on the whole the literature has been sparse on the motivating forces that have created these groups and on their methods of operation.

Harry W. Strachan's efforts to understand the raison d'être of business groups in Nicaragua are the result of a rare constellation of circumstances. The early version of his work was prepared as a thesis for the D. B. A. degree at the Harvard Business School. Happily, the thesis requirements for a degree in business administration allow for a relatively easy bridging of the disciplines. What matters in such studies is an understanding of the problem; any concept that seems to contribute to that understanding, whatever its disciplinary origins, is not ruled out.

Strachan's analysis, therefore, invites the reader to understand the business group in terms that draw from the ideas of organizational theory and microeconomics, with occasional excursions into local politics and culture. His long residence in Spanish-speaking countries and his intimate familiarity with the special circumstances of Nicaragua have made his difficult task a little easier to achieve and his analysis richer and more credible. His work promises to be an important contribution in a neglected field.

ACKNOWLEDGMENTS

It would be impossible to provide a comprehensive list of all those who contributed generously of their time to advise, provide information, criticize, or otherwise assist in the preparation of this study, which was submitted in an earlier version as a partial requirement for the degree of Doctor of Business Administration at the Harvard Business School. Several individuals and organizations, nevertheless, should be cited for their contributions.

I owe a great debt of gratitude to my doctoral dissertation committee; to its chairman, Professor Raymond Vernon, Herbert F. Johnson Professor of International Business Management at the Harvard Business School, for his incisive criticisms, stimulating ideas, and inexorable demands of quality; and to Professors Stan Davis and Rita Rodríguez, also of the Harvard Business School, for their constructive advice and support.

I also owe a great deal to INCAE—Instituto Centroamericano de Administración de Empresas—the school that was my home for the years during which I studied business groups. My colleagues there, Jim Austin, Pedro Belli, Ernesto Cruz, Michael Dean, Dave Korten, Nicolás Marín, Robert Mullins, and Rodolfo Páiz, generously read early drafts and contributed numerous ideas on the subject. The school lightened my teaching load so that I could concentrate on the study, provided secretarial support, and facilitated the interviews. To Giannina Castro, Silvia Román, and Melissa Arellano, who typed numerous drafts, I owe exceptional thanks for great patience and good humor.

I offer my sincere gratitude to the men of business and government who gave much time to the project. Their candor and enthusiasm in answering questions was a great encouragement. To the extent that the description of business groups in this study is accurate, the credit is largely theirs.

Finally, I would like to express a special thanks to Professor Clyde S. Kilby of Wheaton College, who years ago through literature inspired me with awe for the complexities of human activity, and to Professor Lon L. Fuller of Harvard Law School, who in contracts and jurisprudence taught the reciprocal and reverse, and double-reverse aspects of many social patterns. One of the pleasures of the present study in a field far from theirs has been to discover the validity of their ideas.

To my wife, Deirdre, always a loyal and sensitive ally to whom I dedicate this work, my affectionate appreciation.

CONTENTS

LIST OF TABLES AND FIGURES

LIST OF ACRONYMS AND ABBREVIATIONS

AISA
Arquitectos, Ingenieros, S. A.: a local construction firm.

BANIC
Grupo Banco Nicaraguense: a group of financial institutions headed by the Banco Nicaraguense.

CID
Corporación de Inversiones, S. A.: a financial holding company.

INCAE
Instituto Centroamericano de Administración de Empresas: a Central American Graduate School of Management.

INDESA
Inversiones Nicaraguenses de Desarrollo, S. A.: a local financiera.

INFISA
Inversiones Financieras, S. A.: a financiera.

INFONAC
Instituto de Fomento Nacional: the Nicaraguan Industrial Development Bank.

KATIVO
A group of paint and chemical firms in Central America.

SOVIPE
Solorzano, Villa and Pereira: a local construction firm.

"To really understand the financial system of our country," a professor of business administration was telling me, "you must understand that two large groups dominate the Nicaraguan business scene." We were discussing financial practices, but had we been talking about marketing, business, government relations, the formation of new enterprises, or many other aspects of business in this small developing country, his remarks would have been equally appropriate. His basic point was that the business landscape is dominated by large formations called business groups, and that the businessman or economist who wishes to move successfully about this terrain needs to be aware of them.

This intriguing assertion regarding business groups immediately provokes a number of questions:

- Who or what are these business groups?
- How widespread and how important is the business group phenomenon?
- Why do groups exist? What do they do? What functions do they perform?
- What implications do they have for the practice of business?
- What impact, if any, do they have on economic development?

The main objective of this study is to offer some preliminary answers to the above questions. These answers are based on the results of an intensive investigation of business groups in one small country, Nicaragua, in the period 1970-75 as well as on a brief survey of such groups around the world.*

Most studies on business groups (and there are surprisingly few) have preoccupied themselves almost exclusively with demonstrating the economic power that is concentrated in these formations.[1] Implicitly

---

*See Appendix A for a description of the field work and methodology.

or explicitly, the assumption of these studies is that by establishing that a large percentage of the industrial and financial capital of a country is controlled by a small number of groups, the undesirable impact of these groups is also established.

While a measure of the relative size of these associations is an important part of any study, it is clear that a great deal more must be known about how groups operate before conclusions can be drawn as to their impact on commerce and economic growth. An answer to the question, "How do groups function?" probably provides more relevant information for answering, "What is the impact of groups?" than does the answer to "How large are they?" It is for this reason that the main task undertaken in this study has been to describe business groups, analyze intragroup relations, and identify the services provided by groups to their members.

The main arguments of the chapters which follow are summarized below.

DEFINITION

A business group is a long-term association of a great diversity of firms and the men who own and manage these firms. While there are many traits which tend to be common to business groups—family ties, geographical ties, interlocking directorates—three key characteristics distinguish a full-fledged business group from other types of associations:

Diversity of Enterprise

A great variety of enterprises from the industrial, financial, commercial, and agricultural sectors can be found within a full-fledged business group. In Nicaragua, for example, one group has factories making shoes, vegetable oil, and electrical appliances; a construction firm and land developer; breweries and bottling companies; car dealers, department stores, and supermarkets; a bank, finance and insurance companies; an advertising agency; and ranches, sugar plantations, and coffee farms. This diversity of activity, like that found in conglomerates in the United States, suggests that something more than technological economies of scale in production and marketing binds the association together.

Pluralistic Composition

A business group is a coalition of several wealthy businessmen and families. While it is true that each group generally has a leader, and may be labeled with his name, the business group is more than a one-man business empire, more than a single corporation and its vertically integrated subsidiaries, and more than the diversified holdings of a single wealthy family. This pluralism suggests that some positive benefits are necessary to attract distinct interest groups into forming a single entity.

Fiduciary Atmosphere

The relations which bind group members together are characterized by a loyalty and trust similar to the loyalty and trust that is normally associated with family or kinship groups. A group member's relation to other group members is characterized by a higher standard of fair dealings and disclosure than that which generally is found in arm's-length commerce. These close relations among group members provide the potential basis for coordinating activity, and, hence, the concentration of economic power.

SCOPE AND MAGNITUDE

Business groups of relatively great size and prominence in their environments are found around the world. They are particularly noticeable in Latin American countries such as México, Colombia, Chile, Argentina, and Brazil. They are also of great importance in the Far and Near East, in countries like the Philippines, India, and Japan. In the past, groups apparently occupied positions of considerable importance in England, Western Europe, and the United States, although today they do not have the prominence which they once enjoyed in these countries.

The evidence, although limited, suggests that the existence of business groups may well be a phenomenon which correlates positively with the development of modern industrial and financial sectors. This correlation, in turn, suggests that business groups are an organizational form more suited to a developing environment than to a more sophisticated one.

FUNCTIONS AND SERVICES

Business groups come into existence and thrive because of the functions or services that they perform for their members. It is my hypothesis that the principal function provided by a business group is one of financial intermediation, in which the group facilitates both the making of investments for those members with excess savings and the securing of steady credit for those group members with net capital needs.

In addition, groups also help their members maintain a strong market position and provide them with other benefits of concentrated economic power in relation to government agencies, although these group services are of secondary importance. While potentially the associations could, and may in fact, provide operational benefits, such as mutual administrative and technical support, and noneconomic benefits, such as social status, services of these types are not of major importance in the establishment and maintenance of a business group.

IMPLICATIONS FOR BUSINESS ADMINISTRATION

The presence of large business groups in any environment requires that firms both within and without the groups make adjustments in their business calculations. For example, a firm's financial planning and strategy must take into account the impact of group relations on the process of credit allocation; or an analysis of potential markets for a product must reflect the influence of group alliances on buying decisions; or in the negotiations and the design of a competitive strategy, a firm must keep in mind the strength of group relations and the increased resources they make available. Nevertheless, there are a number of pressures or constraints on the business groups which tend to reduce the influence of group alliances on many business decisions. For this reason, the differences in the practice of business within an environment dominated by groups, as compared to one in which they are not present, are minor.

IMPACT ON DEVELOPMENT

The presence of business groups has no clear correlation with the presence or absence of economic development. While it is not likely that business groups have a decisive impact on development, they do make both positive and negative contributions. On the positive side, they contribute to capital mobilization and a more efficient allocation of that capital. They are also among the more dynamic and aggressive elements of the business community in transferring technology and more efficient business techniques to their countries. On the negative side, they reduce competition and contribute to a greater inequality of both power and wealth, with the attendant results of this uneven distribution.

There are good reasons for suspecting that in the early years of the group—the period during which the group is formed—the positive benefits outweigh the negative ones, but that the balance shifts when the groups reach maturity and the country achieves a more industrialized stage.

NOTE

1. Two good examples are Ricardo Lagos Escobar, La Concentración del Poder Económico: Su Teoría, Realidad Chilena, 4th ed. (Santiago, Chile: Editorial del Pacifico, 1962), and R. K. Hazari, The Structure of the Corporate Private Sector: A Study of Concentration, Ownership, and Control (London: Asia Publishing House, 1966). Both are discussed at some length in Chapter 3.

2

DEFINITION AND DESCRIPTION

The principal question to be answered in this chapter is, "Who or what is a business group?" Even though the term "group" appears to be used to refer to associations of diverse firms in numerous countries, such as México, Chile, the Philippines, India, and Japan,[1] there are several difficulties in the development of a definition of business groups that is sufficiently precise to identify and distinguish the object of study, yet sufficiently general for use in comparative studies.

The first difficulty stems from the absence of a body of analytical or comparative academic work on these associations which would have created a precise, commonly accepted definition.[2] To date, most of the work on groups has been descriptive in nature. The writers have generally used the local terminology, examples of which include "los grupos," "los grupos económicos," "financial groups," "investment groups," "enterprise groups," "industrial houses," "las familias," "zaibatsu" (which literally means "financial clique"), and have defined these terms with reference to local phenomena.

A second difficulty comes from the absence on a local level of a sharply-focused definition. The absence of a local definition is well illustrated in Nicaragua. In this country, the label "los grupos" or "los grupos económicos" is used frequently and in a specialized sense by people who participate in or are familiar with the business community.* Yet most of these people have never stopped to define

---

*The specialized use of the term "grupos" has been confirmed repeatedly during the two years I worked on this study in Nicaragua. There have been around 20 to 30 social or semi-social occasions at which I was introduced to a businessman by one of his close friends. At some point in the conversation which followed, I have smiled the smile of an insider and asked, "And what group do you belong to?" The replies, often with the same smile, have been direct, "Oh, I

the term. If asked to do so, they invariably define it by referring to local associations of men and businesses. In other words, they define "group" (the generic term) as "something similar to Groups A and B" (specific entities in Nicaragua). A circular trap is thus created.

The strategy followed in this study to break out of this circular definition consisted of three steps. The first step was to identify those Nicaraguan entities which are commonly regarded as "business groups." The second step was to describe these specific groups and to find out who or what is included in them. The final step was to prepare a list of key characteristics which these associations share in common. The "key characteristics" were then used as the basic definition or criterion for determining the existence of "business groups" in other parts of the world.

A fringe benefit of the methodology followed in devising a definition is evidence that "business groups" in Nicaragua and elsewhere are a sufficiently objective phenomenon to be empirically investigated.

IDENTIFICATION OF THE NICARAGUAN BUSINESS GROUPS

Interviews with businessmen, economists, and others in and out of the business groups revealed that as of 1975 in Nicaragua there are two unmistakable groups, those firms clustered around the Banco de América, those around the Banco Nicaraguense, and a third "special" major group, the Somoza Group, which consists of the enterprises that belong to the ruling family in Nicaragua. In addition there are numerous smaller groupings known as "protogroups," "subgroups," or "grupitos."

Figure 2.1 is a visual summary of these groups and their relations to each other. It reflects the fact that the "grupitos" may be components of a larger group, as is SOVIPE in the Banco de América Group, or may have ties with both major groups, as does the Manuel I. Lacayo Group, or may be largely independent, as is the Terán Group, or may be in the process of forming a major new group, as AISA, INFISA and La Nacional (a Nicaraguan insurance company) appear to be doing.

Figure 2.1 should be read as a static photograph, from 1975, of what is really a dynamic set of relations constantly undergoing modifications.

---

don't belong to any group," or "I suppose I am a member of the Banco Nicaraguense Group," or in cases indirect and evasive. Never, however, has that question drawn a blank stare and the reply, "What do you mean by group?" Similarly, the answer has never been, "I belong to the conservative group," or "I belong to the Nejapa Country Club," or an answer which would indicate that he had understood me to be using the word "group" in some sense other than the one used in this study.

FIGURE 2.1

Nicaragua's Major Business Groups, 1971-75, and a Sample of Minor Groups

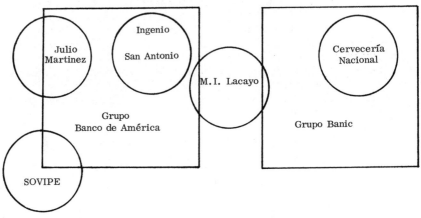

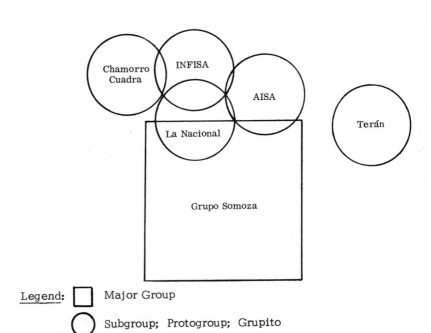

Legend: ☐ Major Group

○ Subgroup; Protogroup; Grupito

Source: Compiled by the author.

TABLE 2.1

Nicaraguan Groups—1971

Question: "What groups currently (Spring 1971) are there in Nicaragua?"

Replies (34)	Number	Percentage
Major Groups		
Banco de América	34	100
Banco Nicaraguense	34	100
Somoza	22	65
Subgroups		
AISA	25	70
INFISA-La Nacional	12	35
SOVIPE	11	32
Lacayo	7	21
Abaunza	7	21
Chamorro-Cuadra	2	9
Other Small Groupings	4	12

Source: Compiled by the author.

Table 2.1 summarizes the percentages of respondents who identified each of the various groups. These groups are described in the succeeding paragraphs.

Banco de América Group

Five distinguishable kinds of businesses were identified with the Banco de América Group. One is an agricultural complex, consisting primarily of the Nicaragua Sugar Estates, Ltd., a large sugar cane plantation established in 1890. The sugar operations have been diversified, and today the Ingenio San Antonio, as it is known, is one of Nicaragua's largest rum distillers and distributors, as well as one of Nicaragua's largest cattle raisers. The Pellas family is the dominant shareholder in Nicaragua Sugar Estates, Ltd., although since its inception, the plantation has been a joint venture among several Nicaraguan families. There are a number of other agricultural ventures, such as coffee farms, which belong to men who are group members, but these enterprises, as we shall see in the section in which group boundaries are traced, are generally not regarded as group firms.

Most of the founding members of the Ingenio San Antonio were merchants. Many of their commercial houses and import-export firms, which continue to be important in today's Nicaragua, are the nucleus of the second type of group businesses, the commercial establishments. In addition to these old commercial houses, some of the most successful new retailers, such as Julio Martínez, an automobile dealer, and Felipe Mántica, an owner of a modern department store and chain of supermarkets, are also members of the group.

A third element in the Banco de América Group focuses on construction and land development. SOVIPE, a complex of firms in the construction industry, is the major subgroup here. SOVIPE began about 20 years ago and is engaged in the production of electrical appliances and construction materials in addition to its more traditional building and land development activities. Since the earthquake, younger elements in the Banco de América Group have formed their own holding company, Santa Monica, which also has become involved in development of commercial centers, recreational activities, and other new ventures.

A fourth component of this group is made up of industrial firms. These include a number of factories which process coffee, produce vegetable oils, and make shoes, as well as some firms of the Lacayo Group.

These agricultural, commercial, construction, and industrial elements are linked together by a set of financial institutions, the fifth component of this group. The Banco de América was established in 1952 by a group of businessmen led by Don Silvio F. Pellas, the uncle of the current leader of the Banco de América Group, Don Alfredo Pellas. Over the years, the bank has grown until today it is the largest private bank in Nicaragua. In 1966, the Wells Fargo Bank bought a minority interest in the Bank, and in that same year founded with the members of the Pellas, the Lacayo, and the SOVIPE subgroups, Corporación de Inversiones, S. A. (CID), a holding company which has interests in several financieras, * a savings and loan association, an insurance company, and several construction material businesses. In 1973 a credit card company, CRED-O-MATIC, now linked with the Mastercharge chain, was established.

Any description of the Banco de América Group would be incomplete without noting that its roots are found in Granada, an ancient city of Nicaragua, and that it is generally identified with the Conservative party in politics. †

---

*A financiera is basically a finance company, popular in many countries of Latin America because it has relatively greater freedom of action than a commercial bank.

†The geographical and, as a result, political orientation of the Nicaraguan groups must be seen against the backdrop of the long and bitter rivalry of the cities of Granada and León in Nicaragua's history. For a brief description of Nicaragua and its history, see Appendix B.

The Banco Nicaraguense Group

The Banco Nicaraguense Group has its roots in León, another ancient city of Nicaragua, and is identified with the Liberal party. Although certain members can trace their relationships back into the nineteenth century, this group is more clearly a product of the last twenty years than the other group.

The distinguishable components of the Banco de América Group have their counterparts in the Banco Nicaraguense Group. A number of members are active in coffee and cotton farming, and several group firms, for example a cotton brokerage firm and a processor of vegetable oils, work closely with the agricultural sector.

Numbered among the Banco Nicaraguense Group are some of Nicaragua's most prominent merchants and commercial establishments. The group is also quite active in the industrial sector. INDESA, the group financiera, has equity interests in a variety of firms including several working with lumber and fish processing. A number of firms established by Dr. Guerrero Montalban, a founder of this group who was also an active industrialist, work closely with the group. One of these, La Cervecería Nacional, the largest brewery in the country, plays a cornerstone role in the group, not unlike that of the Ingenio San Antonio in the Banco de América Group.

The group is also active in land development and construction, but probably on a lesser scale than are either the SOVIPE or AISA complexes.

As in the Banco de América Group, the key firms, those which link the other elements together, are the financial institutions. There are five of these which advertise jointly as BANIC: the Banco Nicaraguense, founded in 1952; a savings and loan association, Financiera de la Vivienda; INDESA; La Protectora, a large insurance company; and a bonded warehouse established at the end of 1973, Almacentro.

The Somoza Group

In 1971, 65 percent of the interviews identified a Somoza business group, although 15 percent of these indicated that it was a special type of group, and not as clearly delineated in the economic realm as in the political. By 1975 there was unmistakable evidence that the Somoza group was taking on many of the characteristics of the other major groups and emerging as a major economic group. Subgroups were forming within it; considerable diversification was taking place; and the firms were beginning to organize themselves more clearly around financial institutions. However, "special" differences, most notably in the access to and use of political power, continue to clearly differentiate this group from the other two in the opinion of most of the business community.

The Somoza Group consists principally of the extensive economic activities of the Somoza family. This family, first in the person of General Anastasio Somoza G., and later in that of his sons, Luis and Anastasio Somoza Debayle, has controlled Nicaraguan politics since 1933. During these 40 years, the family has been an active investor in almost all sectors of the Nicaraguan economy. Today it owns cattle, cotton, sugar, and rice farms. It has equity investments in an airline, shipping and fishing fleets, a cement plant, and a slaughterhouse; its real estate holdings are also extensive.

Since the 1972 earthquake, the group has moved aggressively into construction and land development, into some commerce and into the financial sector with the establishment of the private Banco Centroamericano and an Interfinanciera. The sons of Doña Lillian Somoza de Sevilla have also set up their own financiera. However, many of the credit functions for the Somoza enterprises continue to be performed by the Banco Nacional, the nation's agricultural development bank, which until 1952 was the principal financial institution in the country and is still larger than any of the private commercial banks.

AISA/INFISA/La Nacional

In 1971 approximately 70 percent of the interviewees identified AISA as a group and about half that percentage listed INFISA and La Nacional as a group.

AISA, which was founded in 1958, is a vertically-integrated set of firms in construction and related activities. It has grown rapidly by applying modern techniques to the construction business and by diversifying into areas related to building. In 1963 it established a commercial outlet for furniture and electrical appliances, and later, a joint venture with General Electric to assemble these appliances. Between 1964 and 1966 it established a rock and gravel processor, a factory making wood products such as cabinets, windows and doors, and a firm making concrete products. Diversification began in 1965, when AISA acquired minority interests in a hotel and several other ventures. Around 1970 it began to expand into several neighboring Central American countries as a joint venture partner in large land development and mass housing projects.

From 1973 onward on the crest of the postearthquake construction boom, AISA continued to expand. It also moved out of a special relationship with the Banco Nicaraguense group and helped to establish the new Banco Centroamericano with the Somoza Group.

INFISA, a financiera with interest in firms doing land development, and La Nacional, the country's largest insurance company, owned in part by the government, interchanged stock at the beginning of the 1970s to form what a number of observers call a protogroup. Since 1970

AISA and INFISA and La Nacional have interchanged stock and participated in a number of new joint ventures.

What is perhaps more significant is that some executives within
these institutions are consciously seeking ways to strengthen these
ties and in the process establish a fourth major group. By 1975 several
observers believed that AISA/INFISA/La Nacional was the largest protogroup in the country and only several years away from becoming a major
business group.

SOVIPE

SOVIPE, AISA's principal competitor, was identified by most
interviewees as a "subgroup" of the Banco de América.

Like AISA, SOVIPE began in the 1950s as a construction firm,
prospered by using modern construction and engineering techniques,
and then gradually diversified back into the business of producing and
supplying construction materials. It also established financial institutions, such as a savings and loan association, Inmobiliaria de Ahorro
y Préstamos, to finance construction, and a land development firm to
sell construction projects.

Unlike AISA, in 1971 SOVIPE had no open ambitions to form a distinct major group of its own. It was enthusiastically a member of the
Banco de América Group and was publicly perceived as such. The
association was rooted in family relations between one of the founding
partners of SOVIPE and Alfredo Pellas, current leader of the group, and
had been formally cemented by the formation of a holding company,
Corporación de Inversiones, S.A. (CID), for a number of SOVIPE, Lacayo,
and Pellas interests.

In the postearthquake period SOVIPE has continued to grow aggressively. The entrance into construction of other new subgroups of the
Banco de América, however, has forced it to assume a more independent
stance within the Banco de América Group.

Manuel I. Lacayo Group

In 1971 a third of the interviewees also listed the Manuel I. Lacayo
firms as a business group, although again many of these tended to
describe this formation as a subgroup or grupito. When these interviewees later identified the firms in these groups and marked their
relation to the two major business groups, an interesting and somewhat perplexing pattern appeared—the Manuel I. Lacayo Group is
regarded as a subgroup of both the Banco de América and the Banco
Nicaraguense Groups.

Manuel Ignacio Lacayo, a Nicaraguan engineer and constructer, became a multimillionaire in Venezuela during the decade following World War II. When he returned to Central América, he settled in Costa Rica, but invested his money throughout the Isthmus in a variety of firms. In Nicaragua, a sample of these firms include a hotel, a bottling company, a shoe factory, and a car dealership. Although he had the economic muscle to form his own group and found a bank, he chose instead to work with the two banks which were established in the early 1950s. As a result, he became the largest single shareholder in the Banco Nicaraguense. His brother, Róger Lacayo, was, until his death in 1975, Vice President of the Board of Directors of that bank, and a number of the Lacayo firms which Róger Lacayo directed work closely with the Banco Nicaraguense and are considered part of that group.

On the other hand, Manuel I. Lacayo also became a large shareholder in the Banco de América, and some of his firms, such as a beverage bottler, which are fierce competitors of some of the most important firms in the Banco Nicaraguense Group, established a close working relation with the Banco de América. Lacayo, who was at one time a director of the Banco de América, is now represented on the Board of Directors of this bank by his son-in-law, who is active in those of his father-in-law's firms which are associated with the Banco de América.

Other Grupitos

There were several other associations of firms mentioned as business groups or grupitos or subgroups by 10 to 25 percent of the interviewees. Some of these have already been mentioned in describing the components of the major groups and represent clusters of family-owned enterprises such as the Mantica and Julio Martinez groups within the Banco de América.

Others are largely independent. The Abaunza Group, for example, had a set of paint and chemical firms, although after the earthquake this grupito sold most of its interests in Nicaragua and left the country. The Chamorro-Cuadra Group is a construction company primarily involved with roads and public works, and the Grupo Terán is a set of commercial firms.

There are also a number of regional agricultural groups, primarily from the rich area of Chinandega, which are being wooed into the major groups.

Only a sampling of these grupitos has been included in Figure 2.1. Compared with a major group, each grupito is rather narrow in its activities and small in size, and hence clearly distinguished by the interviewees from the major business groups.

CHARACTERISTICS OF BUSINESS GROUPS

In naming Nicaraguan business groups, the interviewees often cited certain characteristics of these associations, characteristics which they were apparently using as the criterion for identifying business groups. The purpose of this section is to select from among this list of recurring group traits three characteristics which can serve as a definition of business groups and which, in my opinion, also reveal important facets of these formations.

The first signal of a full-fledged group is the existence within it of a great variety of enterprises. In Nicaragua, as we have seen, the typical group spans the agricultural, commercial, industrial, construction, and financial sectors of the economy.

This multiplicity of activities is one way in which a "grupo" is distinguished from a "grupito." Diversity of activity is important for two reasons. First, it allows these groups to reach a much greater size (absolutely and relative to the rest of the economy) than would be possible for firms committed to one area of activity. Secondly, it suggests that economies of scale in production and marketing are not the basis of the group formation. Economies of scale may explain the pattern of vertical integration followed by some of the subgroups like AISA, but they do not explain the relation established between group firms who neither buy nor sell each other significant quantities of their products.

The second distinguishing characteristic of a business group relates to its composition; it is a coalition of a number of different businessmen and wealthy families. We have seen in Nicaragua that while each of the major business groups has its leader, each is much more than a single corporation and its vertically integrated subsidiaries, and each is also much more than the diversified holdings of a single wealthy family.

The Banco de América has the Ingenio San Antonio subgroup controlled by the Pellas family (although this firm began as a venture of several wealthy Granadino families and continues to this day to have a multiple ownership), the firms of Julio Martínez and his family, the Mántica enterprises, the SOVIPE complex, a number of Manuel Ignacio Lacayo's firms, and those belonging to other interest groups.

The same sort of pattern predominates in the Banco Nicaraguense Group. As Dr. Eduardo Montealegre's description of the group's formation in Appendix D makes clear, this pluralistic composition was a deliberate objective. At the time the Banco Nicaraguense was formed, an effort was made to bring into the promoting group wealthy businessmen from the different geographical areas of Nicaragua, from different sectors of the economy, from different political factions, and from different

families. To avoid the disproportionate influence within the group of
any one faction, the promoters agreed to adopt a policy of limiting the
ownership interest of any single person or family to no more than 10
percent.

The significance of pluralism within a business group is that it
leads us to seek an explanation for this phenomenon within the group
itself. Since the group is a coalition of different interests, it is not
explained as simply the byproduct of family or political configurations
elsewhere in the society. It is more likely that its existence is due to
the fact that it is able to provide each of its constituent parts with some
needed services.

The third defining characteristic of a business group is, to borrow
a legal phrase, a fiduciary atmosphere. The relationships among group
members are characterized by obligations of loyalty and fair dealing
similar to those expected among family or clan members. The norm of
intragroup behavior contrasts with the arm's-length bargaining atmosphere typical of the rest of the business environment.

It is not insignificant that a large number of the interviewees, who
by and large had great difficulty in articulating what it meant to be in
a business group, signaled "loyalty and trust" as the main characteristics of a group. As one interviewee stated: "Establishing a climate
of trust is essential to the creation of a group, yet one of the most difficult conditions to achieve and maintain. "

This group characteristic of mutual trust helps distinguish business
groups from looser associations, such as the Nicaraguan Chambers of
Commerce and Industry. This is also an essential ingredient if the group
is to achieve the close coordination of economic activity which results
in a meaningful concentration of economic power. [3]

There are several other traits common to business groups which
were noted with sufficient frequency to merit mention and an explanation
for their exclusion from the definition.

Most business groups reflect strong family and, to a lesser extent,
geographical relationships. In Nicaragua the great importance of these
ties was shown in a number of ways. A number of people used family
names to refer to the group, for instance, calling the Banco de América
Group the Pellas Group. In the section of the interview in which the
respondents classified a list of people by group affiliation, a typical
response would be, "X is a member of the Banco Nicaraguense Group
because he is a brother of A and cousin of B. " Geographical links were
used for similar purposes; for example, "X is a member of the Banco de
América Group because he is a conservative Granadino. " So great is
the importance of family in the groups that one interviewee argued that
the real group is the family group; business groups are simply a mani-
festation in the economic sphere of these family groups.

Two factors, however, suggest that disproportionate weight should
not be laid on the family and geographical characteristics of the business groups. The first is the many clear exceptions which belie any

generalization about families and business groups. It is true that the typical business group is honeycombed with family relations, but it is equally true that there are numerous family relations which cut across group lines. One highly visible example is the relationship which exists between the recently-named chief executive of the Banco de América Group and his father-in-law, one of the key shareholders and directors in the Banco Nicaraguense Group. Similarly, there are several close relatives of the founder and leader of the Banco Nicaraguense Group who were not considered by the interviewees to be members of that group.

These exceptions are also on the increase. As the children of the group founders intermarry (most of them belong to the same social class), the number of intergroup family relations will increase. Were groups a function of family ties, we would expect with the passage of time a blurring of group identity. In Nicaragua, however, group consciousness is greater today than it was 15 years ago, and with the formation of holding companies will probably become even sharper in the future.

A second reason for not stressing family ties as a group characteristic is that this trait fails to distinguish business groups from other types of organizational arrangements in the country. In Latin America, it is natural for family ties to be carried into every sphere of life. Sons are expected to follow their fathers into the same business, and brothers and brothers-in-law and cousins regularly work together; strong family links are found in virtually every business and every complex of businesses. In the major business groups, the presence of family ties is not exceptional; if anything, these associations have made unusual efforts to extend themselves beyond the limitations of traditional family and geographical relations.

Interlocking directorates, and to a lesser extent interlocking stock holdings, are a common characteristic of business groups. The relatively easy access to the names of company directors makes this a favorite defining trait for most researchers trying to identify the groups.[4]

In Nicaragua, where most group firms are sociedades anónimas (the Latin American equivalent of the corporation), it is a common practice for 50 to 100 percent of the directors of a group firm to be trusted group members, either large shareholders of the firms or, increasingly, executives from sister corporations. For example, a study* of the directors of the financial institutions of the Banco Nicaraguense revealed that 13 men occupied 32 or the 55 important director and executive positions in these five firms and virtually all of the key positions on the Board of Directors.

---

*The study was conducted by the author based on information gathered in 1970 on the composition of the board of directors and the Gerente Generales of the Banco Nicaraguense, INDESA, La Nacional, Financiera de La Vivenda, and FINANSA.

While there is no question that the interlocking director is one of the principal means by which the group laces its firms together, the interviewees revealed in their classification of businessmen that membership on the board of directors is far from synonymous with inclusion in the group. Several groups have adopted a strategy of having some "outsiders" on the board of directors; in one, the policy is to choose four of the five directors for a firm from among the group but reserve one position for an outsider the group is eager to attract or whose contribution it values.

A second reason for not referring to interlocking directorates in the definition is the superficiality of this trait. This superficiality is exposed if we consider the situation in which a law is passed prohibiting interlocking directorates. Anyone who has watched the groups in operation knows that such a law, even if implemented, would not destroy nor even seriously impair the important group relations and patterns. [5]

Where the laws encourage the corporate form of business and the atmosphere is not hostile to groups, the interlocking directorate is an excellent first step in identifying and mapping the business groups. However, the researcher should be aware of the dangers of assuming too precise a correlation between group membership and the patterns found in firm directorates.

Thus in this study a business group is defined as an association of diverse firms controlled by a number of different men and families, who have established among themselves a long-lasting relation of trust and cooperation.

BUSINESS GROUPS COMPARED WITH OTHER ORGANIZATIONAL ARRANGEMENTS

The definition given of a business group in the preceding section makes it one species of a genus which includes a number of other types of associations among business firms. Since much is known of some of the other arrangements and since there is also a tendency to confuse business groups with these associations, the following taxonomy is offered.

One interfirm arrangement identified by economists is the multiplant firm, an enterprise which has more than one plant, all producing the same goods and services. A chain of grocery stores or a manufacturer of cans with plants in different states are both examples of multiplant firms. Economies of scale in purchasing, marketing, and administration are the most common reasons advanced to explain why these multiplant forms exist.

Another much-discussed business arrangement is the vertically integrated firm, a business in which a number of entities engaged in successive stages in the production and marketing of a product are brought together under common ownership or control. A textbook example of a vertically integrated firm is a steel company which has subsidiaries to mine ore, others to ship it, still others to smelt it, and finally others to fabricate it. Economies of scale in production is one of the reasons advanced to explain this type of firm. Another is reduced risk. If, for example, a large capital investment requires a steady supply of ore, then control of the ore supplier provides greater power to ensure that the supply of ore is there when necessary and in the amounts required. Downstream distributors help stabilize demand, especially if the industry is oligopolistic.

Similar in many ways to the vertically integrated firm is the horizontally integrated firm, referred to by some writers as a diversified firm. A diversified firm is a business which makes and sells a variety of different products which are closely related either in their production or distribution. A firm selling aftershave lotion, shaving cream, and razors might be one example of a diversified firm. Diversified firms are the result of economies of scale made possible by overlapping production or distribution processes. They also may enjoy economies of scale in research or in management expertise.

Conglomerates are business arrangements which have developed recently, in which a variety of interprises, not generally vertically or horizontally integrated, are brought under common corporate ownership but continue to be run by different management. Conglomerates appear to be primarily creatures of the stock market in the United States, in that their formation is facilitated by the way in which the public values growth companies. There are claims, however, that the conglomerates reduce risk to investors through diversification and serve a useful management service by redressing the distribution of power between salaried management and owners of common stock.

In discussing cartels and trusts one moves from organizational arrangements based on ownership to ones based largely on agreement. When several firms producing the same products enter an agreement to sell at similar prices and perhaps to share the market in certain percentages, they are said to form a cartel. When the same agreement is buttressed by the assignment of voting control of the competing corporations to a single trustee so that he can ensure compliance with the agreement, a trust is created. Both of these arrangements among competitors are designed to facilitate larger profits by reducing price competition. They also reduce risk by assuring each firm a share of the market.

Finally, this century has witnessed the flourishing of many industry-wide or sector-wide associations in both the developed and developing countries. These are organizations, such as the Chamber of Commerce or Industry, for all the businessmen or firms in a particular industry or sector of the economy. Most of these organizations are not designed to set prices or split the market. Their primary purpose is to represent the common interests of the industry or sector before government and the public. They also gather information and do research of

interest to all their members. By facilitating communication among com
petitors and by their ability to influence government intervention in the
sector, these organizations reduce the businessman's risk of ruinous
competition and undesired government intervention.

Where do business groups fit in this schema? Many of the enterprises which are members of a business group are multiplant firms; som
are vertically and/or horizontally integrated. Such firms are usually
identified as subgroups within the larger business group.

Group firms may also participate in cartels and even serve as lead
ers in their creation, but since normally there is only one group firm in
each industry, a business group should not be confused with a cartel o
trust.

In many ways the business group is similar to a conglomerate; both
join under common ownership and control a great diversity of firms.
There are some important differences, however. In the conglomerates,
a common parent owns the subsidiaries but generally few operational or
personal ties exist among the sister subsidiaries. On the other hand,
within business groups, the owners can vary greatly, but there are gen
erally personal and operational ties among all the firms. The conglomerate is easily identified and defined because the relationships among
the firms are legal, whereas the group, being built in many cases on
personal relationships, is much more difficult to delineate legally. Pos
sibly the biggest difference is the way they are formed—the one through
mergers and acquisitions, the other in a more gradual, informal manner
Whether or not conglomerates and groups both tend to reach the same
basic interfirm arrangements along different routes and whether or not
both tend to serve the same ends is not clear. For the time being, ther
fore, it seems best to think of them as different organizational arrangements.

BOUNDARIES OF BUSINESS GROUPS

There is some ambiguity in Nicaragua as to where a group ends.
For example, it was not clear to some of those interviewed whether or
not a cattle ranch owned by a group member should be regarded as a
group firm. The purpose of this section is to explore the borderline
areas carefully to ensure that the picture of business groups being developed rightly describes the phenomenon.

The desire for a precise boundary line comes from academic necessity. In order to measure the extent of a group's economic control, it
is important to be able to distinguish those men and firms who are withi
the group from those without. It is also necessary to know the limits of
a group, in order to know the extent to which generalities about intragroup relations and services are valid. In spite of these necessities,
virtually all of the writers who have set out to study groups in a systematic way have found that the group phenomenon does not easily lend

itself to precise demarcation. However clear the existence of a business group and the the identity of its major members, there are always a number of firms and men whose status in the group is somewhat vague. R. K. Hazari, in describing the Indian groups notes, for example, that

> the group is not always a closed circle. Rather, it may be compared to a series of concentric circles. The innermost circle may be said to consist of the decision-making authority (whether it can be detected straight away or not) which exercises control and influence in varying degrees . . . over the series of outer circles. . . .[6]

The image of the group as a series of concentric circles is an apt one. In Nicaragua, a system in which men and firms could be classified as key, regular, or marginal members seems to reflect accurately the concept of most of the interviewees. At the center of the group are those men who are its leaders and those firms of greatest importance. Next come the regular members, businesses "controlled" by group members which "work with" other group firms, and the influential and trusted men of the group. Firms controlled by group members but not closely integrated into the activities of the group and men with little influence or limited ties to the group are marginal members. Occasionally, there is a "special" case, like that of Manuel Ignacio Lacayo, a man too important to be regarded as "marginal" yet too aberrant to qualify as a regular or key member (see pages 13-14 for a description of the Lacayo subgroup).

As Table 2.2 indicates, in Nicaragua the boundary area of vagueness about the the types of firms in the business group is not great. There is near unanimity that the financial institutions and the nonfinancial firms controlled by these institutions are group firms. Personal businesses are regarded by a majority of respondents as group firms, especially when the enterprise is owned by a very important member of the group or works closely with other group firms. There is nearly unanimous agreement that simple clients of the group firms, such as borrowers from the bank or suppliers to group firms, are not to be classed as group firms.

The agreement of the interviewees in classifying specific Nicaraguan firms was even greater than in their replies to the general question of Table 2.2. Ninety percent of the interviewees classified examples of personal businesses of important group members which also work closely with other group firms as "group businesses." Interestingly enough, a majority still classified a firm which does not do business with the group firms but is controlled by a group member as a group firm.

Figure 2.2 is a visual representation of the relative status of the different types of firms in the Nicaraguan groups.

TABLE 2. 2

Types of Firms Defined as Part of Group

Question: In the Nicaraguan business world, one often hears talk about the groups, for example, the Banco de América or Banco Nicaraguense groups. When you say, "that firm is a part of group X, " which of the following firms might this include?

| | Percent | | |
Replies (33)	Yes	No	Other
1. Commercial Bank X	100	--	--
2. Financial institutions controlled by Bank X	100	--	--
3. Nonfinancial institutions controlled by Bank X and its related financial institutions	93.9	6.1	--
4. Personal businesses of one or several of the directors of Bank X or its related financial institutions	63.7	30.3	6.1
5. Firms with loans from Bank X or its financial institutions	3.0	94.0	3.0
6. Suppliers to or distributors for firms controlled by Bank X	2.9	91.2	5.9

Note: "Controlled" was defined as the power to designate, directly or indirectly, the majority of the board of directors and the top management positions in the firm.
Source: Compiled by the author.

It is even more difficult to draw a precise line between those people in and those out of a group than between firms in and out of the association. In spite of the increased fuzziness of the border area, there still is considerable agreement, as Table 2. 3 demonstrates. In Nicaragua, major shareholders and directors in group firms and chief executives of important group enterprises are regarded by everyone as members of the group. Most of the respondents also consider as group members hired executives and major shareholders without a voice on the board of directors. Minor shareholders and employees are not considered members. The son of an important group member or a trusted consultant is generally included in the group, but an intimate friend of a leader is not.

The comments accompanying the answers in Table 2. 3 and the manner in which specific individuals were identified reveal the criteria of classification. Major shareholders without administrative roles (as directors or executives) and second echelon executives are classified by about 85 percent of the interviewees as group members, if they are "loyal" to the group. Their status within the group, which averages

FIGURE 2. 2

Relative Positions of Group Firms

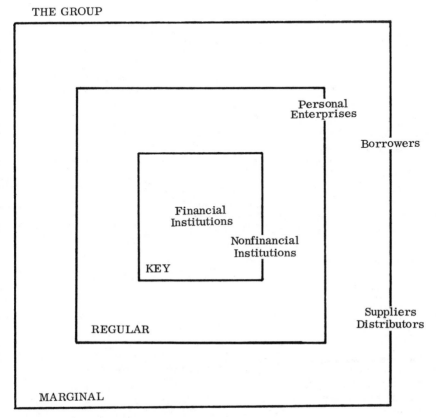

THE GROUP

Personal
Enterprises

Borrowers

Financial
Institutions

Nonfinancial
Institutions

KEY

Suppliers
Distributors

REGULAR

MARGINAL

Source: Compiled by the author.

between marginal and regular, depends largely on their "influence" in group affairs and on how "trusted" they are by the other group members. Sons of key group members who are economically active in the family businesses are regarded as "regular" group members, more because of the future influence they are expected to wield than as a measure of their current weight. A consultant working exclusively with a group is identified within that group, and his status is purely a function of his "influence. " One consultant of long standing received "key member" ratings by a majority of the interviewees even though most of the other consultants on the list of names were generally classed as "marginal" group members. Figure 2. 3 summarizes visually the average status of the different types of members in the Nicaraguan groups.

TABLE 2. 3

Types of Persons Identified as Group Members

Question: When you refer to a person as a member of a group,
this can include which of the people described in the following
list?

	Percent		
Replies (33)	Yes	No	Other
A person who is a shareholder with limited holdings in Bank X or in one of the firms of Group X, who is not a director nor does he play an executive role in the business of the bank or its firms.	11.8	88.2	--
A person who is an important shareholder but who is not a director and does not appoint a director to the bank or businesses of the group.	52.9	47.1	--
A person who is both an important shareholder and director or namer of a director, in the bank and/or businesses of the group.	100	--	--
A person who is an active director, chief executive, or plays a significant executive role in the group, but who is not an owner of equity although he may have a portion of the profits.	97.1	2.9	--
A person who is an executive in the bank or the business of the group but without a share of the profits.	76.5	20.6	2.9
An employee in one of the businesses of the group.	17.7	73.5	2.9
A person who is the son of one of the major shareholders and directors in the group but who is not himself a director or executive or shareholder in the business of the group.	64.7	29.4	5.9
An intimate friend of a major shareholder and director of the group who is not himself an owner or executive in the businesses of the group.	29.4	58.8	17.8
A person who does consulting for the group on a regular basis but is neither a shareholder nor executive in the businesses of the group.	58.8	38.3	2.9

Note: "Executive role" is the translation of "papel gerencial, "
which was defined in the questionnaire as a significant influence in
the operations and direction of the business, not necessarily requiring
formal title or position.
Source: Compiled by the author.

FIGURE 2. 3

Relative Positions of Group Persons

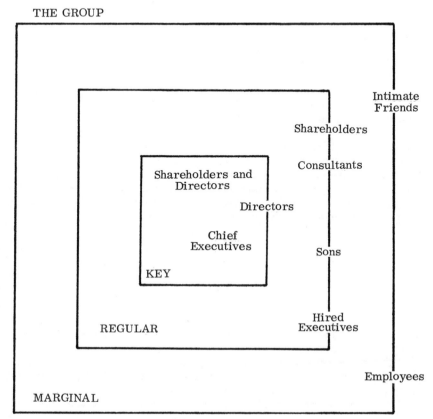

Source: Compiled by the author.

If "control" and "working with other group firms" are the major criteria for determining whether a firm is a part of the group or not, then
"influence" is undoubtedly the major criterion for determining whether
or not a person is a member of the group. This influence can stem from
the ownership of a major block of shares and the ability to turn this
ownership into positions on the boards of directors of various group
enterprises. It can also stem from personal competence and positions
of executive responsibility within the group. In exceptional cases, it
can stem from influence over a key member of the group, as a relative
or trusted consultant of that member.

The nature of the criteria of group membership, as revealed in Nicaragua, makes it clear that there will always be uncertainly concerning the precise point at which a group ends. If, for example, being "controlled" and "working with other group firms" is the measure used to determine whether or not a firm is placed within the association, we can be reasonably sure that there will always be cases in which there is reasonable doubt as to whether a given firm is "sufficiently controlled" or is "sufficiently integrated" with other group firms to be regarded as a group member, since concepts like "control" and "influence" reflect continuums more than sharp divisions. Nevertheless, the Nicaraguan experience also demonstrates that vagueness of the border areas is limited to a minor number of cases, and is much more the result of the difficulties of measuring or applying the criteria than of an innate vagueness in the concept itself. For most Nicaraguans, the idea of business groups is quite clearly understood, even if it is not always known whether a particular firm or businessman meets the requirements. As we show in the section which follows, even with all the uncertainties the application of the idea is sufficiently precise to facilitate meaningful empirical investigation of the business group.

AMENABILITY OF BUSINESS GROUPS TO EMPIRICAL INVESTIGATION

In addition to throwing considerable light on group composition, the interviewees' classification of 54 firms and 90 businessmen provided convincing evidence that the general concept of a business group is applied with considerable uniformity in Nicaragua.*

Table 2.4 summarizes the classification of the 54 firms and reveals that 75 percent or more of the respondents agreed in their classification of approximately 80 percent of the firms.

The high degree of conformity in the answers becomes much more obvious when one notes that a large number of the firms were selected for the list precisely because they represented difficult cases. Of the

---

*Two types of research were conducted in Nicaragua to determine group boundaries. In one, the interviewees were asked to tell what firms or persons should be considered group members. Tables 2.2 and 2.3 give the results of this section. In the other, the interviewees were presented with a list of the names of 54 firms and persons. The lists were compiled to include members of both major groups, minor subgroups and nonmembers. The list also includes a variety of positions in the firms such as shareholders, directors, executives, and consultants. The names in both lists were arranged alphabetically. For more details on methodology, see Appendix A.

TABLE 2.4

Classification of 54 Firms as Group Members

| | Affiliation According to Majority | | | |
Classification	Banco de América	Banco Nicaraguense	Other	Total
Number of firms classified in same group by over 90 percent of respondents	13	12	6	31 (57)
Number of firms classified in same group by 75-90 percent of respondents	4	1	7	12 (22)
Number of firms classified in same group by less than 75 percent of the respondents	4	3	4	11 (21)
Total	21 (40)	16 (29)	17 (31)	54 (100)

Note: Figures in parentheses are percentages of the total.
Source: Compiled by the author.

11 firms (21 percent) which were not classified by 75 percent or more of the respondents in the same fashion, three are firms belonging to the subgroup which is considered part of both groups and which has been described earlier, three more are firms which are the result of joint ventures between the two main groups, two are family firms in which members of the family can be found in both groups, and three are firms where the numerous question marks and the limited number of responses indicated that many respondents did not know the firm.

Of the 12 firms classified by 75 to 90 percent of the respondents in the same way, eight appear to be firms connected with subgroups which are affiliated with, but not completely identified as part of, the larger group. Several were little-known firms, and two were firms identified by ownership with one group but doing business with the financial institutions of the other group.

The impressive degree of unanimity, coupled with the logical explanations for those cases in which there was not agreement, strongly suggests that the concept of group is applied with a considerable degree of precision to firms in Nicaragua.

The agreement among the responses classifying the 90 persons was also high, especially since a number of difficult cases were purposely introduced in the list. The average person on the list was classified by 83 percent of the responses in the same major category, that is, as Banco de América Group, or Banco Nicaraguense Group, or other.

Approximately half of the 90 persons (43) were classified consistently into the same major group by 94 percent of the respondents.

The distribution of the composite index* in Figure 2. 4 gives another measure of how uniform the classification of the people on the list was. If one assumes that groups are a mental fiction and cannot be identified in the real world, then one might well assume that the replies would be randomly distributed among the nine possibilities. With nine alternatives, four with positive values, one with a value of zero, and four with negative values, one would expect to get a pattern of the composite index approximating a normal bell-shaped distribution with a mean of zero and a small standard deviation, since the sample is large (90) and there are approximately 35 replies per person. This is quite a difference from the distribution of Figure 2. 4.

A chi-square test was performed as a means of illustrating the improbability of the pattern of replies which occurred in the classification of the 90 persons, had the replies been associated with one or the other categories in a random manner. The interviewee replies were organized on a contingency table with three columns titled Banco de América, Other, and Banco Nicaraguense, and with 90 rows, one for each person on the list.

If the interviewees had not shared a similar concept of what makes someone a member of a group or if they had disagreed about the application of the concept, one would have expected a random distribution of replies for each name, so that each cell could have had approximately the same number of replies (. 33 x 35). A chi-square test used to calculate the degree to which the pattern of replies did not follow a null hypothesis of random distribution yielded an astronomical X^2 of 3, 570; this X^2 is so high as to be almost absurd. The hypothesis that the distribution pattern is random may, therefore, be easily rejected at the 0. 001 level. [7]

---

*The composite index is simply a weighted average of all interviewee replies regarding a specific individual with the following values given to replies:

3	2	1. 5	1	0	-1	-1. 5	-2	-3
Key	Reg.	Spec.	Marg.	Other	Marg.	Spec.	Reg.	Key
Banco de América Group					Banco Nicaraguense Group			

The absolute value of the index tends to reflect the importance of the person in the group, the sign identifies the group.

FIGURE 2.4

Distribution of the Summary Index of Persons Classified

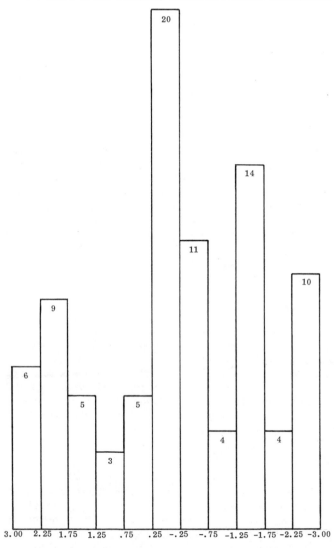

Banco de América Group   Banco Nicaraguense

Note: The Summary Index is the average of all the classifications of a particular person on a scale from 3.00 to −3.00. The larger the number, the more important the person in the group.
Source: Compiled by the author.

CROSS-CULTURAL APPLICABILITY OF THE DEFINITION

The question posed at the start of this chapter was, "What is a business group?" The answer or more accurately the various answers given to that question have all been based on a study of the groups of Nicaragua; it is important at this point to clarify the degree to which they are applicable elsewhere.

The definition of a business group which stresses the diversity of firms, the pluralistic composition, and the fiduciary atmosphere has purposely been fashioned to serve as a universal definition of a business group. It describes or matches accurately the phenomena studied in Nicaragua, and we expect to show in Chapter 3 that it accurately describes a number of associations or formations in other parts of the world.

Whether or not the boundaries of the business groups of Nicaragua are an accurate reflection of boundaries elsewhere is a more difficult question. I expect that business groups in other countries will be found to have a structure similar to that of the Nicaraguan groups, that is, a clearly defined center with a certain amount of vagueness at the fringes. I would also expect to find that the same basic criteria of "control," "working together," and "influence" are used in other countries to separate group members from outsiders, although in any particular country, the outward indicators of that control or status might be quite different. In Nicaragua, for example, membership on the board of directors is a reliable signal of a person's status within the group—in other countries it could easily be something else. * Similarly, because in Nicaragua most agricultural activity is financed by the government bank, and for many businessmen a cattle ranch is more a hobby than a business, the interviewees were reluctant to classify a member's cattle ranch as a group business. But in another country in which agricultural activities are more closely integrated with other group business and not viewed as hobbies, we would expect these enterprises to be automatically classified as group businesses.

---

*Even among the Nicaraguan groups, there is some evidence of differences in the signals of status. Although in virtually all other matters the answers of the interviewees showed no variations consistent with the interviewee's affiliation, it was interesting to note that the Banco Nicaraguense interviewees were more inclined to regard an important shareholder without an administrative role as a group member than were the Banco de América respondents. This difference is easily explained by the much greater frequency in the Banco Nicaraguense of large shareholders who play no active role in the direction of the group's activities.

THE ESSENCE OF A BUSINESS GROUP

Up to this point, we have answered the question, "What is a business group?" in terms of external characteristics. On occasion, as in the section dealing with interlocking directorates or group boundaries, we have been forced to a more abstract level and to the use of criteria like "control" and "influence" in order to reflect local usage, but the objective has been a definition which could be used in empirical work.

A person whose interest is more in understanding how the groups operate rather than in identifying them might come to the end of this chapter and say, "You have told me how to recognize a business group and more or less where it ends, but I still want to know what a group is. What is the essence of a business group?" There is an "essence" definition of a group, which I believe is very useful. Since it is closer to an explanation of groups than a definition, I present it in Chapter 4. In that chapter, I claim that the business group is essentially a network of relationships between the different economic entities (the firms and the persons). These relationships are reciprocal and the motivation for entering them is predominantly economic. Each relationship must be seen as part of a larger network of relations whose design incorporates a business strategy which is, in large part, a response to particular environmental conditions.

This abstract definition leads naturally into a study of the dynamics of these relations and an explanation of how groups are formed. Before proceeding with that examination, however, we consider in Chapter 3 how widespread and important the business group phenomenon is.

NOTES

1. Raymond Vernon, The Dilemma of Mexico's Development: The Roles of the Private and Public Sectors (Cambridge, Mass.: Harvard University Press, 1965), p. 20; Ricardo Lagos Escobar, La Concentración del Poder Económico: Su Teoría, Realidad Chilena, 4th ed. (Santiago, Chile: Editorial del Pacifico, 1962), pp. 161-64; R. K. Hazari, The Structure of the Corporate Private Sector: A Study of Concentration, Ownership, and Control (London: Asia Publishing House, 1966), p. 1; Chitoshi Yanaga, Big Business in Japanese Politics (New Haven, Conn. and London: Yale University Press, 1968), pp. 119-28; "Philippine Life Insurance Co., 11F55," a case published by the Intercollegiate Case Clearing House, Harvard Business School, Soldiers Field, Boston, Massachusetts.

2. Two partial exceptions to this are found in the work of Joe S. Bain and Robert T. Aubey. In his discussions of industrial concentration Bain has coined the term "supercontrol" group for situations in which

individuals, families, or other closely associated groups of persons or influential investment banking firms are in a position to exercise centralized control over the operations of several ostensibly independent corporations. (Joe S. Bain, Industrial Organization, 2nd ed. [New York: John Wiley, 1968], pp. 93-99.) He distinguishes "supercontrol" groups from "general influence" groups built around financial institutions plus a few very wealthy families with widespread industrial holdings. The difference apparently rests on whether or not the group exercises active control and coordination of its firms' operations. (Joe S. Bain, International Differences in Industrial Structure: Eight Nations in the 1950's [New Haven, Conn.: Yale University Press, 1966], pp. 95-96.

Robert T. Aubrey in several articles has distinguished a "second level" of enterprise control and ownership," called "investment groups," from the traditional family firm. These groups "generally include a commercial bank, a financiera, a mortgage bank, an insurance company, and a cluster of industrial and commercial firms. The ownership and control of the investment group is generally wider than that found in the traditional family firm." Robert T. Aubey, John Kyle, and Arnold Strickon, "Investment Behavior and Elite Social Structures in Latin America," Journal of Interamerican Studies and World Affairs 16, no. 1 (February, 1974): 73-95. Robert T. Aubey, "Private-sector Capital Mobilization and Industrialization in Latin America," Journal of Interamerican Studies and World Affairs 12, no. 4 (1970): 582-601.

3. Aubey, Kyle, and Strickon attribute much of the success of the Mexican Investment groups to the network of information which can be mobilized because of the kinship atmosphere within the groups. (Aubey, Kyle, and Strickon, op. cit., pp. 77-89.)

4. Lagos, op. cit., and Hazari, op. cit.

5. There is a similar situation in India having to do with the managing agencies. Although an industrial group was laced together by managing agencies, when legislation limited the usefulness of the managing agency, the group was not seriously affected. (Hazari, op. cit., pp. 11-12.)

6. Ibid., p. 7.

7. Charles T. Clark and Lawrence L. Schkade, Statistical Methods for Business Decisions (Cincinnati: South-Western Publishing Co., 1969), pp. 430-34. The formula for calculating the degree of freedom in a contingency table r X c for purposes of a chi-square test is:

$$d.f. = (r - 1)(C - 1)$$

which would mean there are 178 degrees of freedom in the contingency table described above. "If the degrees of freedom exceed 30, the quantity $2x^2$ is approximately normally distributed with a mean of $2(d.f.) - 1$ and a standard deviation on one. This may be expressed as:

$$z = 2x^2 - 2(d.f.) - 1$$

An application of this formula to the results of the classification of the 90 persons suggests that the pattern of actual results is approximately 65 standard deviations from what one would expect if the replies had been randomly distributed.

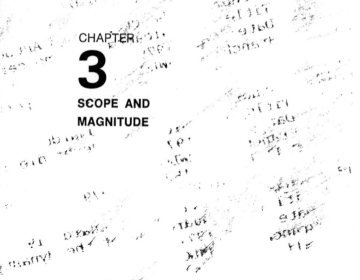

3

CHAPTER

SCOPE AND
MAGNITUDE

The question of interest in this chapter is the extent to which business associations characterized by diversity of economic activity, pluralistic composition, and fiduciary relations are found elsewhere in the world. There are three specific objectives. The first is to identify business groups in other parts of the world insofar as this is possible from a survey of readily accessible materials. This process of applying our definition to phenomena in other environments should clarify the picture of groups.

The second objective is to gain some idea of the magnitude or size of these business groups, as one way of measuring their importance. The final objective is to present as a hypothesis for future research a possible pattern of the time and place in which business groups appear.

The materials of this chapter are arranged geographically beginning with México and South America, moving then to Asia and Europe, returning to North America, and ending in Central America.

MEXICO

On the northern part of the Central American isthmus in México, business groups similar to those we have identified in Nicaragua play a major role in the economy. [1] David H. Shelton's description of these groups notes the diversity within the group and the key role played by financial institutions.

> Financial "groups" consisting usually of a major commercial bank, a strong financiera, and lesser insurance, banking, or similar firms have come to dominate private finance. These groups are often allied with a circle of commercial or industrial firms which absorbs a considerable part of the credit which the financial entities are able to provide. [2]

Professor Raymond Vernon in his account notes many of the family and geographical traits and, implicitly, their pluralistic composition:

[a] dozen or so major groups . . . have been created in México through the linking of the country's principal enterprises. A large proportion of the major industrial and banking enterprises of México belong to one or another of these groups. Nonetheless, though the existence of the groups is an important and indisputable fact of Mexican business life, it is not easy to define them precisely. Each group characteristically incorporates a banking institution or two and an assortment of industrial enterprises. Sometimes a dominant personality or principal stockholder is the chief link among them, as in the case of the Antonio Sacristán and Carlos Trouyet groups; sometimes it is a common major source of credit, as in the case of the Banco Nacional de México group; sometimes it is a community of interest blended of credit sources, family connections, or geography, as illustrated by the complex composed of Monterrey and Banco de Londres y México interests or by some of the smaller groups of the provincial cities. [3]

While a measure of the size of these groups is not available, their importance is well established. Professor Vernon states that the predominance of these groups is a statement to be taken on faith rather than on the basis of statistics:

The aggregate sales of manufacturing firms overtly identified with one or another of the known groups does not constitute a very large part of total manufacturing output, according to our estimates. But the identified firms do tend to dominate the list of the country's larger companies; and the affiliated banks of the identified firms tend to control much of México's private credit resources. [4]

Roberto Dávila Gómez Palacio estimated that, as of 1952, the four major financial groups (each headed by a commercial bank) controlled about 70 percent of the resources of Mexican private financial institutions. [5]

It is my impression, based largely on oral information, that the Mexican groups were formed during the period between the wars and reached their positions of dominance during and shortly after World War II.

SOUTH AMERICA—CHILE

Argentina, Brazil, Chile, Colombia, Venezuela, Bolivia, Ecuador, and Perú are all Latin American countries in which "industrial-commercial-financial" complexes dominate the business scene. [6]

In each of the larger Hispano-American countries—Colombia, Venezuela, and Chile, for example—there appear to be from 8 to 12 major business groups. In countries like Venezuela and Colombia, most of the groups carry family names. On the average, they appear to be older than the Central American groups, reflecting perhaps the greater maturity of the financial and industrial sectors of these countries. Some reached a size, importance, and diversity sufficient to quality them as business groups soon after the turn of the century, although most are probably 20 to 40 years old.

The typical group appears to have grown out of some industrial complex, as for example, textiles in Medellín, Colombia, and then with time diversified into or allied itself with firms in finance and other areas of activity. [7]

In Colombia, I am told, the groups have a strong geographical orientation reflecting the sectionalism of the country. Nevertheless, it is clear that in recent times the Bogotá groups have moved into Medellín and Cali territory, and the Medellín and Cali groups have moved into Bogotá.

However widespread the phenomenon of business groups in Latin America, they are not a subject on which there is much literature, and most of what has been written is in the form of passing references. A welcome exception is Ricardo Lagos' description of the Chilean economic groups in La Concentración del Poder Económico. [8] This book is of special interest not only for the description of these groups and their tremendous influence in the Chilean economy but also for Lagos' argument that they are inimical to development.

Lagos' principal preoccupation is to determine the degree of concentration of economic power brought about by the existence of these groups. Taking 1958 information on sociedades anónimas in Chile, he constructs a list of the firms in each of the eleven main economic groups. A firm is regarded as "controlled" by a group if a majority of its directors are group members. [9] A firm is under group "influence" if one or two of its directors are group members. Concentration of economic power is measured by summing up the capital of those firms "controlled" or "influenced" by groups and determining what percentage it represents of all the sociedades anónimas of Chile.

He finds, as we have, that delineating a group precisely is not easy. Relationships within each group appear in pyramid form—at the bottom, firms join in vertically integrated subgroups; these subgroups are linked into family or multiple family subgroups; [10] and these family subgroups are associated in eleven major economic groups, which appear to correspond to our business groups. [11] The ties among these

11 groups make it possible to identify three federations. Finally, Lagos claims there is evidence that all the groups form one giant "super-group" which controls or influences 22 percent of the total number and 71 percent of the total capital of the sociedades anónimas of Chile. [12]

Among the characteristics of the Chilean groups he documents are several we have noticed in groups elsewhere. Chilean groups generally form around banks and, in fact, many of them take their names from the banks. [13] They are multifaceted and encompass firms active in all parts of the economy—industry, mining, agriculture, and commerce. [14]

Some of the economic groups, such as the Banco de Chile, Banco Sud-Americano, and Banco Español groups, are loosely-knit federations. Most of the firms in these groups have only one interlocking director, so it is quite possible that he serves more as a representative of the subgroup on the bank's directorate than as the agent of the bank on the board of directors of the firm. [15] Others, such as the Banco Edwards, Punta Arenas, Banco Continental, and Banco Panamericano groups, are more closely interrelated, and the probability that the group exercises significant control on firm activities is correspondingly higher. [16]

Some groups formed around a large bank which had already taken a dominant position in the financial system, as appears to be the case with the Banco Chile and perhaps the Banco Sud-Americano groups. The majority, however, appear to have begun with the foundation of an industrial complex and only later founded their own banks. Clear examples of this pattern are the Banco Nacional del Trabajo and Banco Continental groups. [17] Some of the groups are much older than others. The Banco Edwards Group had apparently already formed at the turn of the century. [18] Others like the Banco Nacional del Trabajo and Banco Continental groups are more recent (probably formed after World War II). [19]

Some groups are strongly regional, such as the Punta Arenas groups, [20] but most have spread through the entire country, and there is a noticeable tendency in this direction. [21] In some of the groups, there is no single, dominant leader, but in others, especially the newer ones, such as the Banco Nacional del Trabajo, Banco Español, and Banco Continental groups, [22] one man appears as the clear chieftain and guiding spirit of the group.

Family links are very important in most groups, such as the Banco Edwards and Banco Continental groups; in almost all, there is clear evidence of more than a single extended family. [23] In one, the Banco Español Group, the ties are basically commercial and ethnic. [24] Although Lagos does not specifically note the fiduciary atmosphere, its existence is essential to his argument and assumed by many of his statements about groups.

In a post scriptum written in the early 1960s, Lagos argued that although some of his statistics and relationships among the groups were no longer valid, in general the picture remained the same. [25] Several Chilean economists with whom I have discussed the book, level a more damaging criticism at the work than that of obsolescence. They argue

that Lagos draws very exaggerated claims of control and influence from
the existence of interlocking directors and, in places, clearly inflates
the size of groups by including the same firms in more than one group.
His inferences reach a peak of imagination when he reduces all to one
"supercontrol" group. That Groups A and B have directors in Company X,
which may be a state-created firm, and that Groups B and C are joint
venture partners in Company Y does not make A, B, and C members of a
meaningful supergroup. Neither his methodology nor his doctrinaire
Marxist framework, according to these economists, give him an insight
into the complexity of the economic groups of Chile, and they cause
him to assume that the groups are bigger, more homogenous and coordinated, and more powerful than, in fact, they are. While I find these
criticisms valid, they do not seriously affect the use I have made of
the material gathered by Lagos.

In 1975, after the election of Allende, the nationalization of the
banking system in Chile, and the subsequent coup, the general picture
is radically different from that of the early 1960s. These events, subsequent to Lagos' work, however, have not cancelled the significance
of his study—only underlined it—since one of the reasons for the nationalization of the financial system appears to have been a desire to
dismantle the business groups and to reduce their economic power. (This
point was made by two Chilean economists in separate interviews. One
was active in the Allende government, the other opposed to it.)

INDIA

Across the Pacific, in many of the Asian countries, business groups
also flourish. The only detailed written information I have for this re-
gion deals with groups in India and Japan, so my principal sources for
such a sweeping generalization are fellow students of business administration and economics who have told me of the groups in their own countries. These men from South Korea, Taiwan, Malaysia, and the Philippines claimed that groups are also to be found throughout Southeast
Asia. There are, as well, passing references to groups in writings about
Pakistan and in business administration cases on the Philippines. [26]

In india, where there has been considerable governmental as well
as scholarly interest in the concentration of economic power, two
studies that appeared in 1966 and 1967 provide a wealth of valuable
information on Indian business groups. [27]

Both Drs. R. K. Hazari and M. L. Kothari, whose primary preoccupation is with the "concentration of economic power in the corporate
private sector, " quickly reach the conclusion that the "combinations"
which are critical in India are the "business groups" or "industrial
houses. " Hazari argues that the traditional methods used in other
studies to measure concentration of economic power—the share of the

largest companies in industrial output, the concentration of ownership of share capital, and the concentration of management of companies (through the managing agency system)—have not revealed the locus of economic power. In India, "the unit of control and decision in the corporate private sector is the business group. . . ."[28] Both authors, therefore, tackle the problem of the concentration of economic power on a "group" basis, Hazari through a description and analysis of 20 of the largest Indian groups, and Kothari with an analysis of three of the principal linking devices—managerial integration (various firms with the same managing agency), interlocking directorates, and financial integration. Both studies are heavy with balance sheet information on the groups, primarily from the 1950s, and replete with specific illustrations of the generalizations made concerning the houses.

It is clear that the Indian "groups" or "houses" are very similar to the business groups I have described in Latin America. They are associations which have fanned out into a wide variety of different activities covering the industrial, commercial, and financial sectors of India.[29] They are pluralistic in composition, as the following description makes clear:

> Some groups, moreover, have clusters of companies which function as sub-groups in the sense that the management of the clusters is more or less autonomous and the ownership of shares is not always closely inter-connected with the rest of the group, but their operations generally appear to form part of the group's activities.[30]

Most of the Indian groups have risen to prominence since 1940, although the roots of many of them go back to investments made as early as 1850, as in the case of the Martín Burn group, or as late as the 1930s.[31] Group backgrounds differ but are similar in that many of the groups began with agro-industrial products, such as cotton and sugar, then followed a path of expansion which invariably led them into the financial sector—insurance companies, investment and finance companies, and banks—as well as into a diversity of other industrial activities.[32]

In spite of the abundance of data, the image of these groups remains rather vague. This is perhaps due to the focus in the two studies on firms and the financial information available for them, instead of on people; perhaps it is because these books are written for Indians who are sufficiently familiar with the groups as to not require more background information. Nevertheless, several aspects of the formation behind the firms show through. One is the importance of family relations. Group names appear to be family names; at times, both authors use family names to establish links between firms.[33] In every case in which specific information on the family is given, the groups turn out to be multi-family, sometimes consisting of as many as ten family sub-groups.[34]

Groups also reflect the caste and ethnic structure of Indian society. In his description of groups, Hazari generally identifies them as Brahman, Parsi, or of the Bania community, and so forth, terms which refer to castes or ethnic communities. In addition, most of the groups have a regional base. [35]

All of the groups Hazari describes, with the exception of two, are national, that is, Indian. The two exceptions are the Andrew Yule and Bird Heigler groups, which are European-controlled. Kothari's list of groups has several more European names, but it is not clear to what extent they represent foreigners or long-established Indian residents. [36]

The groups lace their firms together by different means. The most visible and perhaps the most common is that of "managing agencies."[37] The same managing agency will administer a number of different firms. The Tata Group, for example, has nine managing agents which administered a total of 72 companies in 1958. [38] The managing agency is a form of business organization, inherited from colonial days, in which the owners sign a management contract with a managing agency which runs the companies. Other means of control are interlocking directorates and financial integration, that is, integration achieved by having firms purchase each other's shares and make interfirm loans. [39]

Measurement of groups is complicated due to their propensity to enter joint ventures, including partnerships with the government and foreigners. [40] Nevertheless, it is quite clear that these groups are enormous in comparison with other economic entities in India.

The two largest groups, Tata and Birla, accounted for roughly one-fifth of the physical assets of the corporate private sector in 1958. The 20 large and medium-sized groups of Hazari's sample, narrowly circumscribed to those companies in which the group has a majority of the stock (the Inner Circle), still represent 30 percent of the share capital of nongovernment companies in India. More impressive is the fact that Hazari's comparison of the data for 1951 and 1958 indicate that these "inner" group firms grew faster than the average nongovernment companies during this period. When the "outer" group firms in which the group has less than a majority of the capital are included, the greater growth rate of the groups is even more impressive. [41]

JAPAN

The most famous business groups in the world are the zaibatsu of Japan. Over a thousand articles and books have been written about them; they have long fascinated both the Japanese and non-Japanese. Small wonder, given some commonly known facts. The zaibatsu's rise to industrial dominance matches Japan's development into a world power. The zaibatsu provided the industrial muscle necessary for Japan's war efforts. They were dismantled by the Allies as part of the demilitarization of Japan; yet by 1955, ten years after the war, they had somehow regrouped and were once again leading Japan to the highest economic growth rate in the world. They are said to influence nearly every aspect of modern Japanese society and government.

Behind their popular image, the reality of the zaibatsu is a bit more complex and, as one writer has said, is "generally misunderstood in the West."[42] One point of necessary clarification is definitional, for as M. Y. Yoshino writes, "the term zaibatsu has often been used without sufficient discrimination."[43] Another point of debate is whether the prewar and postwar zaibatsu are really the same thing.

The term "zaibatsu" (meaning literally "financial clique") refers to a huge complex of multifarious enterprises owned and controlled by a single family, or group of families, through holding companies at the top.[44] Zaibatsu fitting this description rose to prominence between 1870 and 1940.

Kozo Yamamuro stresses three characteristics of these prewar zaibatsu:

(1) Semifeudal characteristics in that centralized control rests in a Zaibatsu family, which extends its power through strategically arranged marriages and other personal knight-vassal (dedication) relationships.
(2) Well-knit, tightly-controlled relationships among the affiliated firms by means of holding companies, interlocking directorship, and mutual stock holdings.
(3) Extremely large financial power in the form of commercial bank credit, which is used as the central leverage to extend control in all industries.[45]

Yoshino describes them by enumeration:

Actually, zaibatsu should be classified in three different categories. First, there were the Big Four: Mitsui, Mitsubishi, Sumitomo, and Yasuda. The first three were particularly prominent, having well-diversified industrial, financial, and commercial interests; the Yasuda Zaibatsu largely confined itself to financial and banking operations. The group second in importance to the Big Four consisted of a half a dozen or so combines, including Furukawa, Okura, Asano, and others. Most of these lesser combines tended to confine their activities to relatively narrow fields. The third-ranking group comprised those zaibatsu that emerged in the 1930's to meet the specific needs of the military— a group known as Shinko (newly emerged) Zaibatsu. They included Nissan, Nisso, Nakajima, and others.[46]

However defined or described, all writers are agreed that the prewar zaibatsu wielded great economic power.[47] In 1942, the percentage of paid-in capital of the Big Four is estimated to have represented 50 percent of the financial sector, 32 percent of heavy industry, 11 percent of light industry, and 25 percent of other sectors, such as electric, gas, transportation, shipping, land, and import-export commerce. [48]

Once the war was over, the victorious Allies established a reconstruction policy for Japan in which one of the clearly stated objectives was to reduce this economic concentration through "the dissolution of the large industrial and banking combinations which had exercised control over a great part of Japan's trade and industry. . . ."[49] The zaibatsu holding companies were dissolved, and the shares owned by these companies, along with stock held by zaibatsu family members, were liquidated in such a manner that the zaibatsu families lost their holdings in numerous firms and "disappeared even from the list of stockholders of the zaibatsu banks, once the control nerve of their empire."[50]

While the occupation succeeded in severing the control of the zaibatsu families and dissolving the holding companies, it was not successful in breaking up the large firms which comprised the old zaibatsu or in preventing the reconstruction of new complexes of diversified firms, many of which took on the zaibatsu names as soon as this was permitted. [51] "An important and unique feature of Japan's contemporary industrial organization," Yoshino writes, "is the kigyo shudan, or enterprise grouping. "[52] These "enterprise groups" are of two types, in Yanaga's words:

> Those organized around the former zaibatsu and using the old names (Mitsubishi with 38 separate corporations and a research institute; Mitsui with 22 corporations; Sumitomo with 15 corporations) and those held together by large banks (Fuji, formerly Yasuda; Daiichi; and the Industrial Bank of Japan, through which the enterprises in both groups manage their financing).
>
> These groups, known as keiretsu, cannot be described in American business terms. They are not really monopolies since they compete with each other strongly and no one group completely dominates a given field. Actually, they are horizontal groups of companies, each group containing many varied industries as well as a bank, a trust company, insurance companies, a trade company (or companies), and a real estate company. Member companies tend to cooperate with other companies within the group and to compete with companies outside the group. When entering new fields such as atomic energy or petrochemicals, where investment requirements are beyond the capability of any one company in the group, several or most members will combine to finance the venture jointly. The groups vary in cohesiveness. Within each group, the bank is the primary, though not the sole, source of banking support. The group's trading company

handles the sales, particularly trading, and the purchase of raw materials, but not exclusively. Policy coordination is achieved through presidents' clubs, which meet periodically.[53]

The importance of the largest of the enterprise or business groups "may be seen from the fact that the total capital of the firms linked to them has reached nearly 63 percent of the combined capital of all the firms listed in the first section of the Tokyo Stock Exchange."[54]

Writers such as Yamamuro and Yoshino stress the difference between the prewar zaibatsu and the enterprise group or keiretsu of the postwar period. The former were highly centralized combines joined together under holding companies, while the modern-day groups are federations of large firms with widely-held stock, controlled by professional managers.[55] Nevertheless, a person applying the definitions used in our study will conclude that both the zaibatsu and the modern enterprise groups are examples of business groups. The Allies' occupation policy stripped away certain family and holding company links between the firms but it did not change the key characteristics of the association. Both the prewar zaibatsu and postwar enterprise groups are widely diversified. Financial institutions, which were the nerve center of the prewar zaibatsu, are pivotal institutions of the enterprise groups of the 1960s and 1970s.[56]

Both the zaibatsu and keiretsu are pluralistic in composition. While it is true that the prewar zaibatsu were highly centralized and family owned, it is important to recognize that already in the 1930s the number of families involved in the zaibatsu was fairly large—one writer talks of the 11 branches of a zaibatsu family.[57] An article describing the life of Hikojiro Nakamigawa, regarded as the architect of the Mitsui zaibatsu, makes it clear that by the turn of the century the zaibatsu were passing into the hands of professional managers and were composed of strong independent firms and internal subgroups.[58] In the postwar period, when the presidents of the related firms come together in council, they meet as a group of peers. The banks may be group leaders but they do not control the keiretsu. Finally, the coordination of activities and the multiplicity of informal ties before and after the war are testimony of the fiduciary intragroup atmosphere.

As a final clarification, the postwar enterprise groups should be distinguished from two other associations in modern Japan—the zaikai, (business leader clique) and the vertically integrated combines which are the subject when industrial dualism is discussed.

[Zaikai] connotes a big-business power group. It is frequently interpreted more broadly as a synonym for "business circles," "financial circles," and even "business community." More inclusive than zaibatsu, it is nevertheless restricted to big business. . . . Most frequently identified with the term zaikai are the top executives of our big-business organizations (Federations of Economic Organizations, Japan Federation of Employers' Associations, Japan Committee for Economic Development, and Japan Chamber of Commerce and Industry) and executives of the Japan Industrial Club whose board of directors consists of the presidents of the key organizations and the elder statesmen of business, industry, and finance. [59]

The vertically integrated industrial combine consists of a large industrial firm (often a member of an enterprise group) and its satellites. Some of these satellites are "related" firms (kankei gaisha) in which the parent company is a major shareholder or is able to select the top management personnel for other reasons. Other satellites are "affiliated" firms (keiretsu gaisha), firms with links to the parent through ordinary business relations, generally as subcontractors. [60]

WESTERN EUROPE

European business history contains a number of important groupings that share many of the characteristics noted in the business groups of Latin America and Asia. A study of these groups might begin with the merchant princes of Italy, include the konzern of Germany, families like the Rothschilds, and many lesser-known but equally powerful groupings of financial, industrial, and commercial interests that towered over English and European business in the eighteenth and nineteenth centuries. [61]

Are there, however, business groups in modern-day Europe? Do they have the relative importance they apparently once had? Our evidence on this is quite limited. The economist Joe S. Bain, who has spent a great deal of his life studying industrial concentration in the United States and elsewhere in the world, writes of Italy:

> "Super-control" groups as such do not stand out in modern Italy, but there are at least five large diversified private firms each of which has important operations in several industries. Fiat . . . Montecatini, . . . Societa Edison, . . . Olivetti, . . . Pirelli . . . .
>
> None of these private multipurpose concerns has the size and sweep of an important Japanese zaibatsu, but the resulting multi-industry operations do provide a basis for inter-industry integration within the firm and for reciprocal dealing, and these things tend to lessen the degree of intra-industry competition which is associated with given degrees of horizontal seller concentration, as does similar inter-industry integration by government enterprises. [62]

Of France, he says,

> It is hard to identify in France any "super-control" groups
> with organization and cohesion comparable to that found in
> the post-occupation Japanese zaibatsu. There has been
> considerable talk about such groups existing in France, but
> they would seem to represent mainly either general "influ-
> ence groups" built around financial institutions plus a few
> very wealthy families with widespread industrial holdings—
> a fairly common phenomenon in any of the countries being
> studied.[63]

His conclusions receive indirect support from an examination of
several postwar books on business and industry in France. While there
are occasional references to "families" in several of these books, none
of the writers describes associations which might resemble our business
groups.[64] This omission in a discussion of the structure of business in
France would not likely occur in any book about business in México,
Japan, India, or Nicaragua.

A possible exception to the relative decline of groups in Western
Europe may exist in the Benelux and Scandinavian countries. According
to claims of several of the author's friends from that area, groups are
still one of the significant realities of business, although their power
and freedom relative to state institutions is considerably reduced.

NORTH AMERICA

What about business groups in Canada and the United States? For
persons who have always lived and worked in a community dominated
by business groups, it is tempting to assume that business groups are
found everywhere. Many of the Latin Americans whom I interviewed assumed that the present situation in the United States is no different from
that in their own country and cited the Rockefellers, Morgans, and
Kennedys as examples of U.S. groups. Ricardo Lagos in his book on
the Chilean groups refers to a study of the Roosevelt Committee, which
purports to demonstrate that 106 of the 254 largest firms in the United
States, holding 66.5 percent of industrial assets, are controlled by
eight major groups identified as the Rockefeller, Morgan, DuPont, Koeb-
Loeb, Mellon, Boston, Cleveland, and Chicago groups.[65]

Joe S. Bain summarizes the findings of what apparently is the same
study, one made in 1930 of the "200 largest nonfinancial corporations
and the 50 largest financial corporations" in the United States.

> Each of four families or groups was identified as controlling
> several of these 250 largest corporations. The Rockefeller

group was found to have a "working minority" control in six oil corporations and one principal bank, with total assets of over $4 billion, accounting for about 17 percent of the aggregate assets of the 107 largest industrial corporations. The Du-Pont group was found to have similar minority control of the chemical firm Du-Pont de Nemours, and of General Motors, United States Rubber, and the National Bank of Detroit—total assets about $2.6 billion, and about 9 percent of the aggregate assets of the 107 largest industrial corporations. . . . The Mellon group was found to have majority control of four principal industrial corporations, as well as "alliances" through participation of board of directors with nine other giant corporations. The Mather group in Cleveland was found to have "minority voting interests" in four of the largest ten principal steel corporations, as well as majority control of second largest iron-ore mining company in the country. . . . Very roughly, the four groups in question in the 1930's apparently controlled together about one-seventh of the total assets of all manufacturing corporations in the United States. [66]

Several investment banking groups were also identified. "The J. P. Morgan banking interests, as principally represented in the investment banking firm of Morgan Stanley & Co., [had] 'partial control' of 13 major industrial corporations, . . . 12 major utility corporations, . . . 5 major railroad systems, and 5 large banks, with total assets thus controlled of $30 billion. "[67]
In spite of this evidence, when Bain reaches the point of comparing the super-control groups in countries like Japan and India with those in the United States and Great Britain, he says:

And though powerful financial concerns and large holdings by wealthy families are found in both countries, there is a substantial lack of evidence of the importance of real 'super-control' groups, such as might actually control and coordinate the operations of groups of ostensibly independent private firms. [68]

The resistance that someone familiar with industry in the United States has in equating the business groups observed in a country such as Japan or México with the Morgan or Rockefeller groups, when these are defined as encompassing a number of the largest industrial firms and banks, stems primarily from a sense that the distribution of power in these groups, the seat of decision making, the sense of identity of the parties involved, and the closeness of personal relationships and trust found among the members is so different as to make them distinct types of organizational arrangements.

Control is a complex commodity and the fact is that, on the average, the intercompany coordination affected by the interlocking directorships in the United States is much looser and much less comprehensive than the control and coordination achieved by business groups in other countries. [69]

Since 1930, the relative size of the U.S. super-control groups has almost surely been reduced and, to my knowledge, no other groups of greater size have taken their place. While this statement is based on personal impressions, there is a recent study which indicates that the number of interlocking directors, a statistic often cited as evidence of the existence of these super-control groups, has declined over the last 60 years. [70]

Assuming the super-control families and investment banks are not quite business groups, perhaps there are still some other arrangements in the United States which, although not so large nor prominent, do have some of the characteristics of business groups.

Scattered all over the United States, possibly in every city of any size and many which would be considered quite small, there are businessmen who join together in making new investments, who favor each other with their business, who give each other information, and who perhaps own shares of and serve as directors in the same companies (one of which may well be a local bank). It is also quite common in the United States to find different financial institutions, such as commercial banks and insurance companies, working in close harmony and referring business to each other, or to find savings and loan associations, building contractors, and land developers who have also forged long-lasting interrelations.

A number of teaching cases in the field of business administration which describe real situations reveal these links as background information on some financing, manufacturing, or marketing decision. However, I know of no study which attempts to identify and describe these associations or estimate their size and number. It is almost certain that some of them have developed a variety of activities, an absolute size, and an elaborateness of relationships among their members which would qualify them for the label "business groups." It is probable that there are more of these associations than are apparent to the average American. I doubt, however, that their relative importance in the economy, especially in relation to the large corporations, is anywhere near that of the business groups in Latin America and Asia.

NICARAGUA

We return in this final section of the survey to Central America. In Nicaragua, as we noted in Chapter 2, there are two full-fledged business groups—the Banco de América and the Banco Nicaraguense Groups.

Both have developed since 1950, although the roots of one can be traced directly back into the nineteenth century.

Even when these major groups had been defined with reasonable precision, it was impossible to measure their size accurately because of the paucity of reliable data on them and the rest of the economy. As a substitute, a number of the interviewees were asked to estimate the size of the two major groups relative to the rest of the economy.

The interviewees were asked:

> Imagine a table in which the private sector of the Nicaraguan economy is divided into five sub-sectors. Within each sector Nicaraguan firms are classified in one of three sections. Group firms will be one section and will include not only the firms controlled by group institutions, but also those businesses of individual group members which work in a sufficiently close manner with the groups to have a special relation to the group. In the second section will be those firms which are influenced by the groups. This is tricky nomenclature. We don't mean only those firms which are in fact influenced by the groups, but firms where the potential for influence exists, for example, because of outstanding debts to the financial institutions or because the buyer and supplier contracts. In the third category are those firms not in the groups and not influenced by them.
>
> Now imagine an index which measures the percent of activity of a group in a particular sector. In industry, it might be Group A sales divided by sector sales, or in the Financial Sector, Group A assets divided by total assets. This is an index which describes the percent of a sector's business which is done by group firms. Please note that we are not talking about sales to group firms but rather by group firms.

Table 3.1 summarizes the interviewees' replies.

All replies, even though they differed in amounts, showed the dominance of the groups in the finance and construction sectors and their relatively strong influence in commerce and industry.

Since the estimates were clearly subjective and liable to a great margin of error, objective statistics were collected on the financial sector, on which there was fairly reliable data. The results of this analysis contained in Table 3.2, show that the two main groups, including AISA and La Nacional-INFISA subgroups, account for 80 to 95 percent of the activity of the private financial sector and from 35 to 50 percent of the activity of the total financial sector (government plus private financial institutions, but not including the Central Bank, which plays a role similar to that of the Federal Reserve banks in the United States).

The closeness of the estimates generated in the interviews to those which come out of the more objective study indicates that, although the

TABLE 3.1

Estimates of Nicaraguan Groups' Activity
(in percent)

	Finance	Construction	Subsector Industry	Agriculture	Commerce
Group firms (including firms of group members)					
Range of replies	40-90	45-100	15-40	3-60	6-50
Average reply	68	71	25	22	35
Group "influenceable" firms*					
Range of replies	0-40	0-60	0-70	0-40	0-60
Average reply	13	17	39	10	34
Nongroup firms (including foreign)					
Range of replies	5-45	0-35	10-80	20-77	10-59
Average reply	19	12	36	58	31

*Firms which could potentially be influenced by the groups because of family, credit, or client relationships.

Note: The measure of activity for each sector is the percentage of $\frac{\text{Group Firm Sales}}{\text{Total Sales of Private Sector}}$ or a similar index of total assets. Responses = 7.

Source: Compiled by the author.

49

TABLE 3. 2

Nicaraguan Groups' Activity in the Financial Sector
(in percent)

	Index of Activity		
	Total Assets	Total Deposits of Public, Plus Capital	Loans and Investments
Groups' activity in private financial sector	95	79	84
Groups' activity in financial sector, not including Central Bank	41	47	35
Groups' activity in financial sector, including Central Bank	31	43	35

Note: Groups include B. A. , B. N. , AISA, and La Nacional. Withou
AISA and La Nacional the group assets drop from 95 percent to 84 percent of the assets of the private financial sector.

Source: Compiled by the author.

estimates are soft, they are probably as reliable an indication of the
size of the groups in relation to the rest of the economy as can be derived at present.

In Table 3. 3, the estimates of relative size for each sector are put
into perspective in terms of the total economy, revealing that in Nicaragua business groups probably account for around 20 percent of the
gross national product and exert "potential influence" on close to 40
percent. These figures also show that while the groups are heavily com
mitted to finance and construction, in absolute terms agriculture, indus
try, and commerce absorb a larger portion of their activity.

In interpreting these statistics of group scope and influence, two
important factors must be kept in mind. First, the concepts of "control"
or "influence" are used to describe a reciprocal relationship. The more
one discovers connections between the group members, the more
firmly one becomes convinced that control and influence extend both
ways. The banks and the group leaders are powerful, but they are also
subject to strong pressure from their constituents and followers.

Second, it should be clearly noted that the potential for influence
does not, in fact, mean that this influence has been used. Until the
present time, the groups have not even been able to wholly control thei
own operations, much less try to aggressively influence the activities
of other nongroup firms.

TABLE 3. 3

Nicaraguan Groups' Activity in Relation to GNP

Sectors	Sector/GNP X	Group/Sector =	Group/GNP
Direct Activity:			
Finance	.02	.68	.0136
Construction	.03	.71	.0213
Industry	.18	.25	.0450
Agriculture	.25	.22	.0550
Commerce	.19	.35	.0665
Total			.2014

Sectors	Sector/GNP X	Group + Group-influenced Firms / Sector =	Group-influenced Firms / GNP
Indirect Activity:			
Finance	.02	.81	.0162
Construction	.03	.88	.0264
Industry	.18	.64	.1152
Agriculture	.25	.42	.1050
Commerce	.19	.69	.1311
Total			.3939

Source: Table 3. 1, Central Bank of Nicaragua, Informe Anual, 1970.

OTHER CENTRAL AMERICAN COUNTRIES

Each of the other isthmus countries—Guatemala, Honduras, El Salvador, Costa Rica, and Panamá—also has two or three associations
which fit the business group definition elaborated in Chapter 2.

A research project conducted by a graduate student of business administration in each of these countries in the last part of 1971 revealed
the great importance of these associations and their many similarities
to the Nicaraguan business groups. *

---

*In the last half of 1971, a group of M.B.A. students of INCAE began
a survey of each of the Central American countries in order to identify
the "key" institutions in both the public and private sectors and their
management needs. They collected information on many aspects of society, but focused primarily on the business sector. One objective was
to identify the principal groups and subgroups in the business sector—
which men belonged to which groups, which businesses were associated
with each group. Different teams of students conducted the survey in

These business groups are always national; they are composed of and controlled by nationals or country residents. Nevertheless, one of the most important groups in Honduras originally formed around the operation of the Standard Fruit and Steamship Company. Standard Fruit remains to this day an important, though minority, shareholder in group operations.

Most of the business groups in Honduras, Costa Rica, El Salvador, and Guatemala appear to be a bit older than those in Nicaragua. Many are moving into a second generation. As the sons and heirs of the original group members begin to take over the power and wealth, a new set of marriage, friendship, and business relations are overlaid on the original set, modifying to some extent the shape of the groups and promising even greater modifications in the future.

Ethnic groupings—Jews, Arabs, Czechoslovakians, Chinese—are important in several of the countries, such as Panamá and Honduras. Traditionally, these minority groups remained separate from the business groups, but there is some evidence that some of these ethnic elements are now being integrated into the larger business groups.

In some of these countries, the term "grupito" appears to have a wider meaning than the one we have given it. If this wider definition, which includes family businesses, vertically integrated firm complexes and certain ethnic associations is adopted, then each country can be said to have as many as 20 or 25 economic groups. Often, these formations, which in Nicaragua are labeled "grupitos," "protogroups," or "subgroups," are components of a larger business group, but they may be independent. Some are of considerable wealth and importance, in some cases better known than the larger groups of which they form a part.

In one country, Costa Rica, in which law prohibits private commercial financial institutions of deposit, two large business groups have developed around the two leading newspapers of the country. While these groups do not have important financial institutions to serve as the group hub, they appear in other respects to resemble the business groups of their sister countries. Costa Rica thus provides an interesting exception to the general pattern, an exception which takes on importance in view of our hypothesis that groups are basically financial intermediaries. This case will be discussed in more detail in Chapter 4.

---

each country, but they used a common methodology. The methodology for identifying groups was comparable with that of the research I conducted in Nicaragua during the first half of 1971, although the sample of persons interviewed in these countries was smaller and the scope and depth of the survey, of necessity, more superficial. The students were able to identify specific people and firms with each group. The preliminary results of this survey are found in a 400 page report entitled, "Proyecto P, Fase 1," on file in the library of INCAE.

CONCLUSIONS AND HYPOTHESIS

Although much of the information presented in this survey of business groups around the world is fragmentary, there is enough data to support two conclusions. First, the business groups of Nicaragua with their diversity of activity, pluralistic composition, and fiduciary atmosphere are a phenomenon sufficiently similar to the "familias, " "grupos económicos, " "industrial houses, " "zaibatsu, " "enterprise groups, " and "super-control groups" found elsewhere in the world, that an intensive study of these Nicaraguan formations promises information of relevance to an understanding of other clusters. Second, these business groups are of relatively great size and economic importance in the countries in which they are found. Although business groups rarely account for or control more than half of the activity in any particular area, their position of leadership and their relatively great size magnify the influence which they wield. To say that they dominate the private sectors of their countries is no exaggeration.

Finally, the information which we have surveyed reveals a pattern which suggests a very interesting hypothesis. In Central America, the business groups appear to have coalesced in the last 20 years and are still growing. In other countries, such as México, Colombia, and India, the groups seem older, still vigorous although perhaps not growing in terms of relative size. In Japan, the groups are older still, rejuvenated and changed by the trauma of the world war, but still prominent and important. In Western Europe and the United States, business groups have clearly slipped into the background, giving way in influence in giant publicly-held corporations and government.

This pattern suggests the following hypothesis. The business group begins to appear at the time in which a country embarks on the process of industrialization, and during the period when financial institutions are being established. In this environment, they thrive. Later, in an environment of more sophisticated financial institutions, more reliable markets and infrastructures, and more stable political institutions, they lose their relative prominence. In short, business groups are more suited to the economically developing world than to the more developed capitalist environment.

The limited information which we have appears consistent with this hypothesis, with the possible exception of Japan. Japan already has as highly developed an industrial sector as most of the so-called developed countries of Western Europe and North America. It also has a sophisticated, modern financial sector. If we are correct in classifying the "enterprise groups" as business groups, then Japan would appear as an exception to our hypothesis that business groups tend to decline in importance in a modern, developed economy.

I do not know enough about Japan to fully explain away this potential exception, although such an explanation might well argue that the

rapidity of Japan's growth and its social and governmental structure
makes this country a unique case. This hypothesis does give a special
interest to the question of whether business groups are on the rise or
not in Japan, and hence to the following quote from Yoshino:

> Another significant postwar development [is] . . . the decline
> in relative importance of the former Zaibatsu firms in Japan's
> overall industrial economy. They no longer enjoy the promi-
> nence that they had prior to the war. The dissolution meas-
> ures were partially responsible for this. More basically, how-
> ever, as the Japanese economy grew both in scale and
> complexity, a number of non-Zaibatsu firms came to occupy
> key positions in new industries. . . . There is no question
> that businesses belonging to the prewar Zaibatsu are indi-
> vidually and collectively a potent force in the Japanese econ-
> omy, but they are not omnipresent in every phase of it. . . .
>
> What is the outlook for the future? Will the postwar
> version of the Zaibatsu groups become more unified, will
> they stay as fluid and relatively unstructured as they are
> now, or will they fade away altogether?[71]

The answer can only be tentative. Interestingly enough, Yoshino
does not expect the future pattern to be one of greater groups. The existing bank-centered groups may even become less unified:

> There are recent developments indicating that the relationship
> between the city bank and its client firms is becoming more
> fluid. For one thing, the recent growth of many of the major
> client corporations has surpassed the capacity of city banks
> to supply the bulk of the funds they need. . . .
>
> Another very significant development, which may well
> lead to a basic change in the present structure of the bank-
> centered groupings, is the recent government decision to
> issue government bonds. This has created an additional
> source of funds for business enterprises. The traditional
> source from financial institutions, which has played so vital
> a role, is no longer so strategic. . . . It is also important
> to note that the capacity of major corporations to finance
> their capital investments out of their internally generated
> funds—retained earnings and depreciation—has been in-
> creasing. All these factors are bound to alter significantly
> the future pattern of bank-centered groupings.[72]

We do not pretend that the information in our survey of business
groups proves the hypothesis advanced. Nevertheless, it is appropriate
at this time to mention two of the implications of the hypothesis that
have a bearing on our study of group functions. First, the hypothesis

suggests that there are "young" groups and "older" ones, groups in development and others in decline, and therefore, warns against too free an extrapolation of a study of "young" groups in Nicaragua to countries in which they are considerably older.

More important, this hypothesis clearly alerts us to the presence of the dynamic characteristic of groups. Groups are growing, changing organisms, and a study of groups in one particular time and place must try, in so far as possible, not only to describe the current situation but also to uncover the pattern of growth. The reader will note, for example, that in discussing the impact of business groups on economic development, we distinguish the net contributions of a "young" group in a relatively "underdeveloped" atmosphere from that of a more "mature" group in a more "developed" economy.

Chapter 4 presents an explanation of business groups compatible with both the general evidence from around the world and the specific evidence from Nicaragua.

NOTES

1. Robert T. Aubey, "Private-sector Capital Mobilization and Industrialization in Latin America, " Journal of Interamerican Studies and World Affairs 12, no. 4, 1970.

2. David Shelton, "The Banking System: Money and the Goal of Growth, " in Public Policy and Private Enterprise in México, Raymond Vernon, ed. (Cambridge, Mass.: Harvard University Press, 1964), p. 120.

3. Raymond Vernon, The Dilemma of Mexico's Development: The Roles of the Private and Public Sectors (Cambridge, Mass.: Harvard University Press, 1965), p. 20.

4. Ibid., p. 202, notes 1-6.

5. Shelton, op. cit., pp. 160-61, quoting Roberto Dávila Gómez Palacio, "Concentración Financiera Privada en México, " Investigación Económica 15 (1955): 249-61. See also Arturo García-Torres Hassay, "Las Instituciones de Seguros en México: Su Contribución al Ahorro y al Financiamiento del Desarrollo Económico, " thesis Lic., Univ. Nacional Autónoma de México, Escuela Nacional de Economía, September 1964; Antonio Campos Andapia, "Teoría de la Intermediación Financiera y las Sociedades Financieras Privadas Mexicanas, " thesis, Universidad Nacional Autónoma de México, 1962; Frank R. Brandenberg, "A Contribution to the Theory of Intrepreneurship in the Developing Areas: The Case of México, " Inter American Economic Affairs 16, no. 3 (Winter 1962): 3-23. A possible explanation for the difference in numbers of groups is suggested by these descriptive studies which identify 9 to 12 groups in México but indicate that as a result of coalitions, they can for some purposes be regarded as three or four major groups.

6. Frank Brandenberg, The Development of Latin American Private Enterprise (Washington, D. C.: National Planning Association, Pamphlet 121, 1964) (Brazil, Colombia, Argentina, Chile and Perú); José Luís de Inaz, Los Que Mandan (Buenos Aires: EUDEBA, 1964); and in passing, Tomás Roberto Fillol, Social Factors in Economic Development: The Argentina Case (Cambridge, Mass.: M. I. T. Press, 1961) (Argentina).

During the three years of work on this study in Cambridge, Central America, Venezuela, and Colombia, I have had the opportunity to talk with numerous businessmen, economists, and students from South America. Rarely have I met businessmen and economists who could not talk in considerable detail about the economic groups of their locality. I have heard in this way of business groups in Bolivia, Ecuador, Perú, Chile, Colombia, Argentina, and Brazil.

In addition, I have conducted more formal interviews with businessmen, bankers, and government economists in Colombia and Venezuela: in Bogotá, Colombia (May 1970); Medellín, Colombia (August 1971); and Caracas, Venezuela (January 1971).

7. See Brandenberg, op. cit., p. 30-31.
8. Ricardo Lagos Escobar, La Concentración del Poder Económico: Su Teoría, Realidad Chilena, 4th ed. (Santiago, Chile: Editorial del Pacifico, 1962).
9. Ibid., p. 122.
10. For example, the Banco Sud-Americano is an economic group composed of three large subgroups—Alessandri, Salfa, and Cooperative Vitalicia, as well as several "independents." Ibid., p. 125.
11. The eleven groups identified are: Grupo Banco Sud-Americano, Grupo Banco Chile, Grupo Banco Edwards, Grupo Punta Arenas, Grupo Banco Nacional del Trabajo, Grupo Grace-COPEC, Grupo Banco Español, Grupo Banco Continental, Grupo Cosatan, Grupo Banco Crédito e Inversiones, and Grupo Banco Panamericano. (Ibid.)
12. Ibid., pp. 161-64.
13. Lagos notes three exceptions, although it is interesting that the list of firms of these "exceptions" contains a number of financial firms such as insurance companies. Ibid., pp. 121, 143, 150.
14. Ibid., p. 124.
15. Ibid., pp. 125, 140, 151.
16. Ibid., pp. 122, 140, 142-43.
17. Ibid., pp. 148, 154.
18. Ibid., p. 143.
19. Ibid., pp. 146, 155.
20. Ibid., p. 146.
21. Ibid., p. 123.
22. Ibid., pp. 149, 153, 155.
23. Ibid., pp. 142, 143, 155.
24. Ibid., p. 153.
25. Ibid., pp. 175, 179.

26. Hanna Papanic, "Pakistan's New Industrialists and Business-men: Focus on the Menons, " Conference on Occupational Cultures in Southeast Asia, University of Chicago, May 15-16; 1970; "Philippine Life Insurance Company A, ICH 11F55 PC 54" and "International Oil Company A, EA-R 444" (Boston: Intercollegiate Case Clearing House, Harvard Business School).

27. R. K. Hazari, The Structure of the Corporate Private Sector: A Study of Concentration, Ownership, and Control (London: Asia Publishing House, 1966); M. L. Kothari, Industrial Combinations: A Study of Managerial Integration in India Industries (Allahabad: Chaitanya Publishing House, 1967).

28. Kothari, op. cit. , p. 34; Hazari, op. cit. , pp. 3-4.

29. Hazari, op. cit. , pp. 306, notes 5-7; Kothari, op. cit. , p. 49.

30. Hazari, op. cit. , pp. 6, 305.

31. Ibid. , pp. 69, 213.

32. Ibid. , pp. 69-75, 159, 213, 315; Kothari, op. cit. , pp. 5, 75, 103.

33. Hazari, op. cit. , p. 263.

34. Kothari, op. cit. , pp. 6, 75, 125.

35. Hazari, op. cit. , pp. 159, 212, 263.

36. Kothari, op. cit. , p. 127.

37. Groups in Indian usage generally refer to firms under the same "managing agencies. " Hazari argues strongly, however, that managing agencies are really the management departments of the groups and not the real seat of power. They are a prominent means of control in the industrial sector, but not among the private companies or the financial companies of the group. Even in the industrial sector, this form of organization is on the decline and, if abolished by law, would not significantly affect the power or control of groups. Hazari, op. cit. , pp. 11, 322-66.

38. Ibid. , p. 325.

39. Ibid. , pp. 70, 307; Kothari, op. cit. , p. 41.

40. Kothari, op. cit. , pp. 121-37; Hazari, op. cit. , p. 316.

41. Hazari, op. cit. , pp. 16-22.

42. Kozo Yamamuro, Economic Policy in Postwar Japan: Growth Versus Economic Democracy (Berkeley and Los Angeles: University of California Press, 1967), p. 110.

43. M. Y. Yoshino, Japan's Managerial System: Tradition and Innovation (Cambridge, Mass.: M.I.T. Press, 1968), p. 119.

44. Chitoshi Yanaga, Big Business in Japanese Politics (New Haven, Conn. and London: Yale University Press, 1968), p. 37.

45. Yamamuro, op. cit. , pp. 110-11.

46. Yoshino, op. cit. , p. 119.

47. Ibid. , pp. 119-22; Yamamuro, op. cit. , pp. 112-19; Yanaga, op. cit. , p. 38; Seymour A. Broadbridge, Industrial Dualism in Japan (Chicago: Aldene Publishing Co. , 1966), Chapter 3.

48. Yamamuro, op. cit., p. 114, taken from HCLC, The Japanese Zaibatsu and Their Dissolution, Data Volume, p. 469.

49. Yamamuro, op. cit., p. 2, quoting State of Post-Surrender U.S. Policy, September 22, 1945; see also Yoshino, op. cit., p. 123; Yanaga, op. cit., p. 35; Joe S. Bain, International Differences in Industrial Structure: Eight Nations in the 1950's (New Haven, Conn.: Yale University Press, 1966), p. 85.

50. Yamamuro, op. cit., p. 11.

51. Yoshino, op. cit., pp. 123, 129; Bain, op. cit., p. 87.

52. Yoshino, op. cit., p. 118.

53. Yanaga, op. cit., pp. 38, 39. See also Yoshino, op. cit., pp. 128-48, where 30 to 50 firms are said to be members of each group.

54. Yoshino, op. cit., p. 142.

55. Kozo Yamamuro, "Zaibatsu Pre-War and Zaibatsu Postwar," Journal of Asian Studies 23 (1964): 539-54.

56. Yoshino, op. cit., pp. 129-48; Yamamuro, op. cit., pp. 112-15; Hugh T. Patrick, "Finance, Capital Markets and Economic Growth in Japan," N.Y. University Conference on Capital Markets and Economic Development, January 1970.

57. Hidemasa Morikawa, "The Organizational Structure of Mitsubishi and Mitsui Zaibatsu, 1868-1922: A Comparative Study," Business History Review 44, no. 1 (Spring 1970): 62-83.

58. Tsunehiko Yui, "The Personality and Career of Hikojiro Nakamigawa, 1887-1901," Business History Review 44, no. 1 (Spring 1970): 39-61.

59. Yanaga, op. cit., p. 32.

60. Yoshino, op. cit., p. 148; see also Broadbridge, op. cit.

61. Broadbridge, op. cit., argues that the zaibatsu phenomena of 1887-1940 was a speeded-up version of the banking/industrial process in England and America, and cites several authorities to support his argument.

62. Bain, International Differences, op. cit., pp. 101-02. By "super-control groups" he means two types of associations—those created when "single individuals, families, or other closely associated groups of persons have controlling stock interests in several ostensibly independent corporations," and those created when an "influential investment banking firm" has "'a common influence' over several corporations by virtue of the fact that members of the banking firm are more or less continuously members of the boards of directors of each of the corporations in question." (Joe S. Bain, Industrial Organization, 2nd ed. [New York: John Wiley, 1968], p. 93.)

63. Bain, International Differences, op. cit., pp. 95-96.

64. Henry W. Ehrmann, Organized Business in France (Princeton, N.J.: Princeton University Press, 1957); John Sheahan, Promotion and Control of Industry in Postwar France (Cambridge, Mass.: Harvard University Press, 1963); John H. McArthur and Bruce R. Scott, Industrial Planning in France (Boston: Division of Research, Graduate School of Business Administration, Harvard University, 1969).

65. Lagos, op. cit., pp. 9-10.

66. Bain, Industrial Organization, op. cit., pp. 94-95.

67. Ibid., p. 97.

68. Bain, International Differences, op. cit., p. 80.

69. Bain, Industrial Organization, op. cit., pp. 95-97. For a book giving a current picture of director power and influence in the United States, see Miles L. Mace, Directors: Myth and Reality (Boston: Harvard Business School, 1971).

70. David Bunting and Jeffrey Barbour, "Interlocking Directorates in Large American Corporations, 1896-1965," Business History Review 14, no. 3 (Autumn 1971): 317-55.

71. Yoshino, op. cit., p. 137.

72. Ibid., pp. 139, 146-48.

4

**FUNCTIONS AND
SERVICES**

In this chapter we come to the heart of this study. Having described and defined business groups, the task is now to explain them. Why do groups exist? What services or functions do they perform for their members?

The hypothesis elaborated and defended in this chapter is summarized in Chapter 1 in two propositions. First, business groups are formed to provide their members with certain services. Second, of the many potential functions which a group can perform, the most important are the financial intermediary services connected with securing credit and making investments.

Before we discuss the hypothesis, however, it is helpful to step back and make explicit the framework behind these statements. This chapter begins, therefore, with a conceptual model of groups in which each service or function is seen as a strategic response to certain environmental conditions. After a discussion of some of the most important environmental differences between a developed and developing country, the five principal types of potential group services are examined for evidence of the extent to which groups actually perform these services, and, in so far as they do, the value or importance of these functions for the members.

A CONCEPTUAL FRAMEWORK

A useful image of the business group is to picture it as a bundle of relationships or as a complex system of linkages among certain businessmen and firms. Some of the linkages are explicit and formal, such as those embodied in interlocking directorates or interlocking stock ownership. Others are informal, though no less important, such as the fiduciary bond felt between investors who have worked together over the years in different projects. This focus on relationships and the dynamics of relationships suggests a number of insights into the process by which groups are formed and the conditions which such an association must satisfy if it is to survive.

First, the business group comes into existence, not with the formation or growth of any single firm, but rather when a number of firms, which are already established, begin to develop a special set of interrelations. Although, of necessity, we speak of group members and group enterprises, it is important to keep in mind that, in essence, it is the network of relationships forged among these people and firms which comprises the group.

Since these relationships form gradually, it can be quite difficult to establish the exact date on which a group is born. Many of the firms in the Nicaraguan groups were established 20 to 80 years ago; the groups, nevertheless, have only formed in the last 15 to 20 years.

Second, as most relations are constantly undergoing modifications, the group itself is also constantly changing. This constant change underscores the importance of thinking about groups in dynamic rather than static terms. Expecting change, we ask if there is a pattern to this change. Do business groups have a life cycle? What happens as groups move from the first to the second generation?

Relationships, almost by definition, are reciprocal. Generally, the parties to a relationship receive something they value in exchange for something valued by the others. This rather simple idea of reciprocity is pivotal to the explanation of how and why groups develop.

Parties create among themselves certain relationships which they expect will be mutually beneficial. Over a period of time, these relations are maintained and expanded as the expected benefits materialize. At some point, a group consciousness of these links develops, giving them stability and reinforcing them. The group is born, but the process continues. If a time comes when the parties no longer receive benefits or if the cost of these relationships begins to seem too high, then the parties modify or terminate them. In summary, the business group, as an entity, is formed to provide certain services; it survives and thrives as it is perceived as performing these or other new functions more effectively or at less cost than alternative structures; and it begins to die when it ceases to be able to meet the needs of its members.

This notion that groups are formed to provide reciprocal benefits immediately suggests some fruitful avenues of investigation. What are the critical relations or links that create a group? Who are the parties to these relations? What is it that these parties want from the relationships? What makes it possible for the group to satisfy all of them?

Before following up on these questions, however, it is appropriate to pause and ask whether, in fact, groups are a sufficiently independent phenomenon to be governed by the process of adaptation described above. The question might be raised as follows: Is it not possible that economic groups are simply a side effect of family, political, or social relations and that an examination of the reciprocities within the group misses the critical causal factors?

This is an important question, since our study of groups is, in large part, designed to uncover the services or benefits which groups provide their constituent members. The fact that the group is a voluntary, pluralistic association helps provide an answer and suggests rather conclusively that business groups are not simply side effects of other relations within a society. That parties with distinct interests compose the groups and that their participation in the group is voluntary (membership when offered can be accepted or rejected, and also later abandoned), only makes sense if we assume mutual reciprocities.

In returning to the main discussion it is unnecessary to spend much time discussing who the parties are and what the critical relations are which link them together in a group. It is fairly obvious from the first three chapters that the parties of interest are the group members—the diverse firms and the men who as owners, directors, and managers guide them. Also, the key relations are those which cause these diverse firms (and the interest groups behind them) to think of themselves as a business group and to work together. The picture of groups as an accretion of relations formed over time suggests that initially the key relations will probably be between people, but that, in time, they will be replaced by institutional ties among firms.

What do these owners and managers want from the groups? The motivation of these key members, that, in my opinion, does most to explain their participation in a group, is a desire for economic gain. This is not to say that the desire for power, social prestige, and friendship do not contribute to the formation and maintenance of groups, but rather that without the element of economic gain the groups never would have been formed and would shortly come apart or change into something else.

While an appreciation of the social and familial ligaments of the groups is important to any understanding of a group, it is probable that the primary purpose of business groups, from the point of view of their members, is to facilitate the making of money. The very name and the principal activities of the group suggest as much. There is other evidence. There are examples of groups which have continued to exist when the noneconomic circumstances were changed radically. The prewar zaibatsu in Japan were indistinguishable from the families who owned and controlled them. The occupation not only temporarily dismantled the zaibatsu but permanently separated them from the families who had been their owners. Yet five years after the war, the disparate firms were resuming their previous zaibatsu names and functioning very much as a group, although by this time the families played virtually no role in them. [1]

In Nicaragua, family and geographical ties are strong in the groups. Nevertheless, as we noted in Chapter 2, during the past ten years while each group's sense of identity has increased, most of the family, social, geographical, and political ties, which in their inception distinguished the groups, have grown increasingly blurred.

How does the business group provide its members with economic benefits? An answer to this question takes us back to emphasize a different aspect of group relations, namely their interconnectedness, and to an analysis of the environment in which groups are found.

The group does not consist of isolated relations but of a network of interdependent links. The businessman, considering the decision to enter a business group, weighs the benefits and obligations of all the relationships together, not individually. He does this because the network of links is a single whole; it expresses a coordinated strategy.

Critical to understanding any strategy is an appreciation of the environmental conditions for which it is designed. The environment, consisting of the physical, social, and political constraints under which persons seek to realize their objectives, determines what services or functions are needed, the value of these services and, finally, the relative efficiency of different organizational arrangements that can supply them.

In other words, to explain groups we must look not only at what groups can do, but at what needs being done. The section which follows deals with some of the characteristics of the typical group environment and the needs they create; the succeeding section considers how groups meet these needs.

ENVIRONMENTAL CONDITIONS

Most of the business groups identified are found in countries in the process of industrialization. There are four characteristics of the developing environment to which business groups may be an adaptive response.

First, the developing world is generally a world of uncertainty and considerable ignorance, an environmental condition reflected in the preoccupation of the group member to find ways of reducing his risk of loss. Uncertainty is a part of life everywhere, but the uncertainties of the developing world are of greater magnitude and in some cases of a different character than those in the developed world. The behavior of the government, for example, is less certain. It is said that in countries like the United States, all are treated equally under the law. There is a strong legal tradition against the use of government power in particularistic ways, that is, against the making of laws which treat similar entities in distinct manners. This is not generally the case in developing countries.

There is also greater uncertainty for the businessmen in developing countries in which the government is actively experimenting with a variety of schemes for stimulating economic growth. In one period, the government may channel a number of resources into making import substitution profitable, and then later switch policies to promote exports. The risks appear greater because there is no history of successfully sustained growth to give an optimistic hue to uncertainty in a developing country. There is also greater uncertainty since the use of rational decision making and modern information collecting techniques is limited; rational planning often reduces risk but, even when it does not, it tends to make uncertainty more manageable by clarifying the dimensions of risk.

In such a world of uncertainty, the value of insurance against loss greatly increases. If associations like business groups provide this valued service, they should prosper.

Secondly, the developing, like the developed, world is one of constant change, change which both threatens the businessman and provides him his opportunity. Simon Kuznets sees the key characteristic of this current age as the application of science to production. This revolutionary trend swept England, Europe, and the United States in the eighteenth and nineteenth centuries and has during this century made itself felt in virtually all the countries of the world. It brings with it industrialization, rapid population growth, and urbanization. [2]

The alert businessman living in this world of new products and new techniques of production becomes aware that to survive and prosper is to ride this wave of change skillfully, to locate oneself in the growing businesses and to stay abreast of the new technologies. He also learns that a great variety of inputs are required to take advantage of the opportunities—capital, knowledge and influence, to mention only a few. Some organizational means of amassing and coordinating these inputs is necessary.

When industrialization and the modern techniques arrive in an underdeveloped country, the organizational means available to coordinate the necessary inputs are not usually available. There has not been time nor the need to develop a variety of suitable arrangements. More importantly, the arrangements are limited because the base of social roles, contractual customs, and legal patterns in the society used by these organizational arrangements have not yet been adjusted to the condition of the changing world. If the business group, incorporating as it does many of the traditional familial patterns and relations in the society, is capable of amassing and integrating the necessary inputs, it should be particularly well-suited to take advantage of the opportunities in the transitional environment. Later, however, when the social and legal patterns of a society catch up with the needs of the new structures, it is quite possible that other organizational arrangements may prove more efficient and displace the group.

Third, the world of the potential group member is generally one of small, imperfect markets. Most of the developing nations are quite small; even in the poorer countries with many inhabitants and much territory, the effective market is generally limited; one efficient plant will often produce all that can be sold. This smallness, combined with a number of other environmental characteristics, often contributes to monopolistic or oligopolistic conditions in these markets.

Constant change itself is one of the factors contributing to the imperfections in the market. The stream of new products, the rapid population increase, the migration of people, and their expanding incomes all contribute to variations in the demand for certain products and lags in the adjustment of supply to this demand. Government boundaries and tariffs designed to protect industries also add to the imperfections. The alert businessman in this environment is aware that exploiting the natural imperfections or opportunities of the market, preserving them, and even creating them, as for example through protective tariffs or cartels, is one strategic route to high rates of return on investment. If the business group provides this businessman with leverage on the environment and information on opportunities, its usefulness to him increases.

Fourth, most developing countries are marked, if not by capital scarcity, certainly by underdeveloped capital markets. The differential among interest rates is much greater than in the developed countries. Nonprice considerations are of critical importance in securing credit. In some countries with inflationary tendencies, the interest rates which government and monetary authorities specify that banks shall charge certain sectors are negative once inflation is allowed for. Yet in these same countries, nonbank credit to the same clients, even when adjusted for inflation, can run upwards of 20 percent. Not only is the cost of capital more variable, but it appears that the return on investments is also more variable. Opportunities to open lucrative businesses which have already proven successful in other parts of the world are everywhere. Yet the litter of business failures is also great. If business groups can provide the businessman with credit and investment outlets, they become valuable organizational arrangements.

POTENTIAL GROUP SERVICES

The list of ways in which a group might provide valued services to its members is long. The research in Nicaragua focused on a number of these which had been suggested in the literature and in a preliminary survey. They have been grouped together for convenience under the following categories.

Financial Intermediary Services

One potential benefit of group membership is cheaper, more reliable credit. Two ideas are included here— economies of scale in financing and a greater efficiency in reducing risk. As a result of its larger size, the group makes it possible for all its members to secure credit from outsiders at a lower average cost than would be possible if they worked alone. Also, built-in diversity reduces the total amount of working

capital required for contingencies. Furthermore, the atmosphere of loyalty and the abundance of knowledge about each other reduces the perceived risks associated with capital transfers and, therefore, the risk
premium demanded in intragroup loans and investments.

Attractive investment opportunities is another potential advantage
of group membership. The group brings together in a favorable atmosphere men with diverse ideas, talents, and the resources essential to
the establishment of successful new businesses. Through the group,
each member is thus able to participate in a greater number of more profitable investments than he would otherwise have.

One investment opportunity of special interest in most developing
countries is the joint venture with a foreigner or the dealership of im-
ported goods. It is possible that group affiliations enhance a person's
attractiveness as a joint venture partner and hence his competitive position in securing such participation.

Marketing Services

There are two ways in which membership in a group may help a firm
capture a larger share of the market, stabilize the demand for its products, or create market agreements and conditions which protect attractive margins. One way is by creating a tradition of intragroup business.
The group member in need of a service or good always acquires it from
a fellow member, as long as he suffers no price or quality disadvantage.
(He may even receive a special discount.) The group member selling the
good or service knows he can count on a loyal and perhaps stable cli-
entele around whom he can build a higher volume/lower average cost
business than he would otherwise have. Everyone benefits, and if the
intragroup business reaches sizeable proportions, the group achieves
the economies of vertical integration.

A second way in which the group might help its members in the marketing area is by helping establish market agreements and conditions
which reduce competition. We have already noted that the business
group is not itself a cartel or marketing arrangement, since it rarely has
more than one firm in any particular activity. Nevertheless, it is possible that the power position of the group might enable its members directly or indirectly to reduce competition.

Benefits of Concentrated Economic Power

Both the financial intermediary and marketing services mentioned
above rest in part on the group's concentrated economic power. There
are several other potential benefits, which come directly from the pooling

of resources. It is quite possible, for example, that as a result of the group's network of family and friendship contacts and its contributions to political parties, each member enjoys especially good treatment by the government.

A second possible benefit of association may be preferential treatment from nonmembers. As a popular song puts it, one of the advantages of being in the "in-crowd" is that "you get respect from the people you meet." It is possible that this respect or desire to incur group favor translates itself for the particular member into lower prices and better credit terms on the goods he buys, prompter payment of receivables owed him, and clients who would not normally give him their business.

Operational Services

Are there any operational economies of scales or services which give the group-affiliated firm an advantage over its independent competitors? Economies of scale in production or distribution, such as one finds in vertically and horizontally integrated firms, seem unlikely (other than in certain of the subgroups), given the diversity of group enterprises. It is possible, however, that in an environment in which trained personnel are scarce and the absolute size of all firms is relatively small, the group may supply specialized administrative and technical support of a quality no single firm could afford.

Groups may also achieve economies of scale in the procurement of information. Since the group is composed of people plugged into different parts of the economy and government, it can function as a wide-ranging information system. In this system, members exchange important pieces of information on business opportunities, local economic conditions, international trends, competitor activity, and governmental plans which, if secured by other means, would be much more expensive.

The group can also provide adversity insurance or help in time of trouble. If something happens to the chief executive of a firm, the group can fill the vacuum rapidly. If a particular group member (firm or person) runs into financial adversity, members of the group can help him. For each member, presumably, the value of having insurance is worth more than the premium paid in providing support to the others in their need.

A special instance of the benefit above is the service which a group might provide in solving the thorny problem of succession in a family business. If a member dies before his sons are old enough to take over the business, or if the sons should have neither the aptitude nor the desire to run it, the group may provide an organizational framework which can guide a family firm through the transition period and in this manner preserve the patrimony.

Noneconomic Benefits

In the developing world where economic roles are not sharply differentiated from other roles and where economic power is closely linked to political power and social status, it is probable that an association such as the business group will serve a number of noneconomic functions. If the group is largely identified with the elite, then it is quite possible that a self-made businessman will value participation in the group for social status.

On a more personal level, the psychological benefits of group activity, such as the comraderie of joint action, may be a strong motivation to the group's formation and maintenance.

Finally, for those in pursuit of a political position, the group may provide not only an economic foundation for launching a public career but also visibility and an image of serious leadership, which increase the likelihood of success.

ACTUAL GROUP SERVICES

That the groups might logically provide a certain service does not tell us whether groups, in fact, provide these services nor whether the services are of value. An important part, therefore, of the field work in Nicaragua was to determine which services a group performs and how the group and potential group members value these services. The main research tool, as we have noted previously, was the structured interview, in which a sample of thirty-five Nicaraguan businessmen evaluated and ranked the group services discussed above for the two principal groups. (For a detailed description of the field work in Nicaragua, see Appendix A.) The dynamics within the Somoza Group and the benefits accruing to this group from its privileged position in the government were thought to be sufficiently atypical that the research was concentrated on the more common nongovernmental groups.

In capsule form these interviews revealed that in Nicaragua, credit and investment opportunities are clearly the most important group services, but that the group's role as a broker of joint-venture marriages is minimal. Intragroup business is of clear importance for a majority of the members, but most members feel that the group plays no appreciable role in the control of competition. While the concentration of power is recognized as a key reason for associating, few give the group credit for producing economic benefit in the firm of government business, more efficient government service, or preferential treatment by nongroup persons. What is of some importance is the protection a group provides a member from hostile discriminatory action on the part of government or other economic entities.

Help in time of trouble is a minor benefit. There is little evidence of administrative and technological support within the group or that the groups have played an important role in solving the problem of succession. The group does serve as an information network, but the value of this service also appears minor. For a minority, the social status of group association is important. Psychological benefits play an important role in keeping the group together, but it is hard to imagine that they are responsible for its formation.

Table 4.1 shows the ranking of nine potential benefits cited by the interviewees. In the following sections the evidence for the existence of these potential services is discussed at greater length.

TABLE 4.1

Ranking of Potential Advantages by Interviewees
(Responses = 30)

Potential Advantages	Order of Ranking	Ranked in Top 3	Average Ranking
Sources of financing	1	26	1.9
Vehicle for investment of funds	2	22	2.6
Business of other group members (only 23 in sample)	3	12	3.8
Social and psychological benefits	4	14	4.1
Business relations with foreigners and joint ventures	5	3	5.0
Control of markets (only 5 responses)	6	0	5.4
Support and administrative and technical help	7	5	5.6
Political benefits	8	2	5.9
Preferential treatment by those not in group	9	1	6.2

Note: Five different subsamples ranked a list of nine potential group benefits. Three of these subsamples, representing members of the Banco de América Group, members of the Banco Nicaraguense Group, and nonmembers, did so after a long structured interview. Two other subsamples did so in the process of completing a written questionnaire. One of these represented students, most of whom had experience as executives before returning to graduate school. Table C.1 (Appendix C) demonstrates the importance given to credit and investment opportunities by the executives and students who were not included in Table 4.1. Table C.2 facilitates the comparison of the rankings by subsamples and illustrates the unanimity with which credit and investment were ranked most important.

Source: Compiled by the author.

Financial Intermediary Services

Evidence from a number of different sources supports the hypothesis that credit and investment functions are the two most important services performed by the business group. Outward appearances, for example, suggest the centrality of the financial role in the typical group. In México, Chile, and Japan, the groups are often called "financial groups," and in some cases are known by the name of their leading financial institution. [3] Wherever groups are found, the presence and prominence of financial institutions within them is a recurring theme.

When the viewer moves up closer to examine the organization of the business groups, the financial institutions are almost always found in the pivotal position. In the prewar zaibatsu of Japan, for example, banks were "the central nerves of the holding company operations."[4] These "banks and other former zaibatsu systems came to occupy an even more crucial position in the postwar era."[5] The explanation given for this by Yoshino is that in the reconstruction period the needs for capital were great, but capital markets, such as the stock exchange, were not well developed at that time. As a result, commercial banks and other financial institutions became the principal suppliers and facilitators of capital. In this situation, in which 75 percent of the typical industrial firm's assets were financed by debt, it was not surprising that they clustered together around the financial institution, their solidarity strengthened by cross-firm loans and investments. [6]

The pattern in Nicaragua is quite similar to that in México, Chile, and Japan. Business groups never really formed there until the financial institutions were established; the two major business groups are known by the name of their bank, and the bank president or chief executive in each of these groups is the recognized group leader.

Outward appearances, however, are not enough. The hypothesis implies that businessmen within the group receive, or think they receive, more credit, or cheaper credit, or surer credit than they would get if not associated with the group; it also implies that investors have more and better investment opportunities as part of the group than otherwise. The results of the Nicaraguan interviews clearly demonstrate that the typical group member, and especially the nongroup businessman, believes that, other things being equal, the group member can secure more credit, often at a lower interest rate, than can nongroup businessmen, be they local or foreign. * While it is exceedingly difficult to

---

*The interviewees were asked about four hypothetical situations in which the following issues were raised: amount of credit to a group firm, cost of credit to a group firm, amount of credit to a person associated with the group, and cost of credit to that person. In each situation, the group-affiliated firm or person was compared to a local unaffiliated

measure this credit advantage, several interviewees estimated that the advantage represented 5 to 50 percent more credit for the group member.

It is important to keep this evidence in perspective. The replies are conditioned on "other things being equal," whereas, in reality, they rarely are equal. In neither group do members get loans automatically. In both groups, the financial institutions consider carefully the amount of collateral, the soundness of the firm, and a number of other factors which, according to one bank official, receive more weight in the final decision than does the fact of group membership.

While it was impossible to determine whether group members take advantage of this service to get proportionally more credit from group institutions, a study by Professor Nicolás Marín, using 1968 financial information, suggests that there is little evidence, if any, that group firms' debt represents a greater percentage of their total assets than the debt of nongroup firms. In his sample of group and nongroup firms in the "Food Processing and Beverage" section of the industrial sector, the average debt to total assets ratio for group firms was 43 percent, as compared with a 47 percent ratio for nongroup firms. (See Table C.6, Appendix C.) However, the limited size of the sample, the fact that the average group firm was several times larger than the nongroup firm, the variability of accounting practices in Nicaragua, and the softness of the underlying data which was taken from tax returns caution against the temptation to use these statistics as strong evidence for any conclusion.

Just as there is a common belief in Nicaragua that a group member receives preference in the allocation of credit, so businessmen in and out of the groups believe that the group member has greater investment opportunities due to his membership than he would otherwise have, and that these opportunities are probably among the more profitable and secure investments in Nicaragua. * The group member participates in some of these automatically, as the firms in which he has an interest expand, diversify, and make investments. There is also a custom that when a new project is started, the member is invited in on the group floor, although there is nothing automatic about this. In one group, there are

---

firm, a foreign firm, and a member of another group, similar in all respects (size, industry, and profitability).

Tables C.3 and C.4 (in Appendix C) show that 88 percent of the interviewees felt the group firm gets more credit than the unaffiliated firm, but that only 27 percent believed this credit comes at a lower interest rate. Table C.5 shows the same pattern with respect to a person affiliated with the group.

*As Tables C.7 and C.8 indicate, over 90 percent of the interviewees consider a group member to have more investment opportunities than an outsider, and 75 percent consider those more profitable investments. It was interesting to note, as Table C.9 illustrates, that outsiders (Other) tend to credit the group with supplying even more investment opportunities than do the members themselves.

several instances of members who were left out of new projects to make room for new persons coming in with more important inputs for the group.

Not every other possible financial service is yet exploited by the Nicaraguan groups. A majority of interviewees did not believe that working capital needs are reduced because of group membership, largely because working capital management is far too primitive to take into account group relations.

Also, whether the business group appreciably aids its members in creating joint ventures remains unclear. In India, M. L. Kothari noted the rapid growth of joint ventures between the Indian "business groups" and foreigners during the postindependence period. [7] In Costa Rica, a leading economist and business consultant is of the opinion that the group's primary function is to serve as a marriage broker between foreign firms and local partners. We thus expected that the Nicaraguan case would demonstrate a high percentage of joint ventures and a high valuation of this benefit of group participation. [8]

To our surprise, group members did not seem more active in joint venture than those outside the groups, perhaps even less active. Also, most businessmen in Nicaragua do not consider group membership much of an asset for the person looking for joint-venture partnerships. *

An examination of the Indian situation from a purely statistical point of view suggests a similar situation. At least in 1958, the percentage of joint ventures between group members and foreigners was not much higher than one would expect from the percentage of group firms in the total economy. [9]

Among the explanations for this phenomenon given by the interviewees, the most interesting is that the issue of control tends to neutralize whatever other advantages a group might have. The groups wish to control the enterprises in which they participate and generally have the muscle in negotiations to insist on a majority share. Frequently, the foreign interest wants the same position of power. As a result, the number of joint ventures consumated between groups and foreign firms does not appear significant enough to postulate some special advantage of groups in this type of activity.

A final word remains to be said about the Costa Rican business groups. These, it will be recalled, are groups which appear to be quite similar to the groups in the other Central American countries, except that they do not have commercial banks of financial institutions of credit, since all financial institutions of deposit have been nationalized in

---

*"Joint ventures and commercial dealings with foreigners" was given a uniformly low rating as a potential benefit, as can be noted in Tables 4.1, C.1, and C.2. Among the comments on this point were some which stated that joint ventures were not that widespread in Nicaragua and those that existed were largely established by INFONAC, the national development bank.

Costa Rica for the last twenty years. Is the existence of business groups in Costa Rica an exception which disproves our hypothesis or at least modifies it? Not enough is known about these groups yet to settle the issue conclusively. The following point is mainly one of clarification. The hypothesis, it must be remembered, is that groups perform financial intermediary services, such as credit distribution and the channelling of investment funds, not that the group has financial institutions of its own. Instead of disproving the hypothesis, it is possible that the Costa Rican groups provide interesting examples of a group which channels savings into new investments and loans from one firm to another by means especially adapted to the unusual conditions of Costa Rica. If so, this would illustrate the hypothesis that the group itself—not just the financial institutions within the group—is a financial intermediary.

In summary, the existence of a preference for group members in both credit allocation and participation in new investments seems fairly clearly established in the Nicaraguan case. Similarly, there is little room for doubt that these are the two most important services which the group performs for its members. In Table 4.1 these two benefits were ranked first and second by almost all the interviewees (in and out of the groups). They received equally high ratings in a questionnaire which was completed by middle-level executives and M.B.A. students who had worked in, and were familiar with, the Nicaraguan business scene (see the note to Table 4.1).

Marketing Services

Intragroup Business

Intragroup business appears to be an important and common characteristic of groups everywhere. In Japan, Yoshino reports:

> The relative importance of reciprocal dealing within the member firms has varied from group to group. One prominent Mitsubishi executive estimates that a fourth or a third of the total business of the Mitsubishi group is done among the twenty or so major member firms. If the secondary affiliated and related firms were to be included, as much as a half of the total business could be reported as being done within the total group. It is also estimated that about a third of the total business done by the Mitsubishi Shoji (the group's trading company) consists of transactions within the Mitsubishi group. Although these are crude estimates, they are nevertheless indicative of the degree of mutual dependence in day-to-day business transactions among firms with common prewar Zaibatsu ties. [10]

In Nicaragua, this obligation is called "preferencia en situaciones de igualidad" (preference under equal circumstances). A group member in need of an article or service is expected to give his business to his fellow group member or one of the group firms, other things like price and quality being equal.* The volumes of this intragroup business, however, do not appear as significant as they apparently are in Japan. While the amount of such business varies from firm to firm, most interviewees felt that only in rare cases does it reach or exceed 5 percent of a firm's total sales. Nevertheless, business referrals, which are a form of intragroup business, are quite important for some of the financial firms. For example, the land development and construction company will refer clients to the sister insurance company for fire and life insurance and to the group savings and loan association for credit. In some cases, the referrals may even be forced, as in the following example mentioned by one respondent:

> The developer, one group firm, sells the land on credit and obtains a first mortgage. The new owner of the land, wishing to build a house, can borrow money for that purpose from a savings and loan bank. The savings and loan bank, however, wants a mortgage on the house and property. The developer will yield his first mortgage to the savings and loan bank if it belongs to his own group but not to the savings and loan bank of another group. This encourages the owner to use the group's financial institutions to finance his house.

Control of Markets

In discussing the role of the business groups in the formation of cartels, price support agreements, and other arrangements designed to reduce competition, it is important to distinguish the issue of the existence of these arrangements among group firms from the question of the function which business groups perform in creating or maintaining them.

It is common knowledge to anyone working in Nicaragua—and I imagine that in this respect Nicaragua is quite representative of almost all developing countries—that there are numerous arrangements and conditions at work to reduce competition. The small size of the country is one such condition; a population of two million is simply not enough to support more than several plants making any one product, and in many

---

*Next to "credit," "business to other group members" was the most frequently listed privilege or obligation of group membership. When faced with a specific buying decision, the majority of interviewees, as Table C.10 in Appendix C reveals, consider it an obligation to prefer another group member, but not at any personal disadvantage.

cases the market is too small for even one plant. Monopolistic or oligopolistic situations, therefore, are almost inevitable. Similarly, government policy at both the national and the Central American Common Market level is designed to reduce the number of firms in areas in which it is felt that a proliferation of small companies will lead to cut-throat competition and inefficiency.

Nor is there a tradition of social disapproval of market agreements, which might lead to government policies to reduce them. In the international area, quotas and agreements stabilize prices for export products such as coffee and meat. In the agricultural sector, private associations are generally formed to regulate prices and production, and in cases in which these have not proved effective, the government often sets up an agency to do the job. In commerce, gentleman's agreements not to wage price wars are common, and the ability to design and negotiate a good agreement is regarded as an important management skill.* Similarly, skill in blocking the potential entry of competitors is the mark of a shrewd businessman.

The question, therefore, is not whether there are arrangements which restrain competition in these countries—there are, and group firms and group members participate in them—but whether the groups serve to increase or to reduce competition.

The evidence in Nicaragua suggests that business groups have not directly used their economic power, for instance as credit allocators, to prevent the formation of new enterprises and to eliminate existing ones. This is in large part due to the strong competition which currently exists between the two major groups. One government official who was generally hostile to business groups, when asked if groups reduce competition answered, "Not so far. The groups are prompting the formation of many new businesses. They are both helping and permitting the newcomers to get started. . . . Up until this point, they have not tried to squash them."

---

*One merchant told me with pride of the way he used the "break-even" financial analysis as a device for preventing a price war in his particular area of business. He had been getting reports that certain stores were cutting prices and reducing their margins and that others were beginning to retaliate. Before this degenerated into a price war, he invited all his competitors to his house one evening and, after they had had some drinks, asked each of them what sort of return they wanted on their investment. With this information, he then showed them that their total investment and the volume of business that there was in the country required margins of a certain amount. Any reduction in this margin in order to increase volume could only draw retaliation followed by the loss of that increased volume and reduced profits for all of them. They saw his point and a gentleman's agreement on what the margins should be was the result.

In my opinion, this is an accurate statement. It implies that the direct effect of the groups in Nicaragua has been to increase, not decrease, competition. This is largely the result of the fierce struggle which exists between the groups. There appears to be a strong tendency for each group to try and match the other group; if one begins a financiera, the other does. This pattern of parallel development exists not only in financial institutions, but in land developers, supermarkets, car dealerships, and breweries.

Competition leads the groups not only to compete with each other but also to compete for the business of independents and newcomers, a factor which makes the groups among the elements of the business community most open to new business projects and ideas. Competition in the area of credit has also made them aggressive in the pursuit of new clients and solicitous of the needs of new firms.

Indirectly, however, the effect of the groups probably is to reduce competition. One of their principal motives in the current courting of newcomers and outsiders is defensive. The groups are eager to prevent the formation of strong centers of economic power that could challenge them. Once a person is incorporated into the group, there are pressures on him not to establish firms which would compete with any already owned in common or individually by other members. True, there are competing firms within the groups, especially in the commercial area, but most of these predate the formation of the group or the assimilation of its owner into the group. The group itself follows a clear investment policy of "complementarity" and "noncompetitiveness," avoiding the establishment of firms which compete with the businesses of the group. Thus, in the long run, the group is likely to reduce competition by reducing the number of potential competitors.

Another deterrent to the establishment of new firms is the knowledge that the group gives their own firms preference under equal circumstances, and the possibility, even if remote, that at some critical juncture in a competing firm's existence, a competitor might get the group to cut off credit or use its power in some other way to destroy the firm.

While I have no evidence of any trends, I suspect that as groups grow older, their tendency to use power to reduce competition increases. The Nicaraguan groups are relatively young and have probably not reached this stage. In the future, as the social and family links between them increase, the temptation to use the association of the group to protect investments and profit margins will probably increase.

For the present, however, the conclusion is that currently the groups play only a minor role, if any, in helping their members reduce competition and control markets or prices. This situation was clearly reflected in the relatively low rankings given this potential group service. Table 4.1 shows that, for the majority of interviewees, this was a nonexistent or unimportant group service.

Benefits of Concentrated Economic Power

Several group members when asked why they belonged to a business group answered, "Well, in unity there's strength." In this section, we attempt to trace the ways in which this concentration of power translates itself into tangible benefits for group members and the importance of these benefits.

Political Power

In Central America, as in most of the rest of the world, the businessman is aware that the government touches on his business affairs at many different points, and that good treatment by the government is worth money and, in many cases, costs money. It is possible to provode a long list of specific examples, but perhaps more useful to think about three types of political advantages that membership in a group might provide.

First, the government has in its power the ability to confer many direct forms of economic benefit. It buys a whole spectrum of products and services from the private sector; for example, buildings, roads, desks, and machines. In Central America, the government also allocates export quotas, licenses and special tax statuses. A businessman seeking government-related business might feel that his association in a large group gives him an advantage in securing this business because other group members are influential in government or because the government will be trying to secure the favor of his group. As a member of the group, the government may perceive him as a responsible businessman who can deliver efficiently what he contracts to do and therefore will give him its business.

There is a second way in which the government can affect a man's profits. The businessman is dependent on the government to perform efficiently a number of functions, such as granting operating permissions, customs release, and import licenses. These are presumably given to all who meet certain impersonal requirements. Nevertheless, in obtaining these documents, government red tape, inefficiency, and delays can cost the businessman money. A businessman might believe that his importance and connections are enhanced by being in the group and thus make it more likely that the clerks and bureaucrats will serve him well. They are well aware that the group member has sufficient power to effectively communicate and protest inefficiency in their performance to their bosses as well as to help them when necessary.

Third, the businessman is aware of the many ways in which he is vulnerable to mistreatment by an enemy well-placed in government. If the businessman is not defended against such a possibility by legal traditions and court procedures, he might feel that a close association with other powerful businessmen provides him with some insurance against an attack. To the degree that the enemy cannot attack him personally without attacking the others, there is a built-in deterrent.

Hence, to a greater or lesser extent, businessmen all over the world have to preoccupy themselves with learning how to influence their government favorably, if for no other purpose than simply to ensure that the government performs efficiently and justly the functions that have been entrusted to it. In developing countries, businessmen may have to preoccupy themselves with these matters to a greater extent than is usual, given the general inefficiency of government and the personalistic tradition in which laws can be tailored individually. The degree or extent to which the groups serve the functions of aiding the businessman in securing the government treatment he desires was the point of inquiry in this area.

Only a slight majority of the Nicaraguan interviewees believed that the group members get contracts and efficient government service (the first type of government benefits) at a lower cost and effort than do non-group businesses. Almost all of the interviewees, however, felt that a group member is better protected against particularistic discrimination (the third type) because of his group alliances.* (This conclusion is limited of course to the Banco de América and Banco Nicaraguense Groups. The Somoza Group represents another type of organization in which the monopolies, preferences, and business steming from the political power are believed to be the principal source of the group's economic strength.)

Nevertheless, a number of those who felt that there is a correlation between group membership and good treatment by the government saw no causal link. Good treatment by the government, as more than one person explained to me, stems from the personal relation which a businessman has to those in government, not from the fact that one is a member of a particular group.

Whatever good treatment is received by the one group on account of group membership is, according to most interviewees, also received by the other (even the group which is historically identified with the conservative party, which is not in power). A fairly clear picture of the dynamics is revealed in the following statement by a member of one group:

---

*The responses to the question in Table C. 11 (Appendix C) can be interpreted as indicating a slight correlation between group membership and good treatment from the government. From the breakdown of these governmental advantages in Table C. 12, it is clear that the groups' main advantage vis-à-vis the government, is that they are better defended against particular discrimination. Eighty percent of all the interviewees indicated that there was some advantage to being in a group in regard to this point.

I have answered indicating no preference for our group but in several instances preference for the other group. The difficulty in answering stems from being specific on the "cost and efforts" of getting things from the government. We all go through the red tape and applications. By being more solvent and having a multiplicity of friends, groups might have an advantage. We do have more friends in the government, so you might think we would have greater preference. But that is not the case. Our friends feel they must be impartial. Also, they feel that by giving a preference at times to those of the opposition, they neutralize the opposition. They don't really help their own. . . .

An indirect way of examining the degree to which business groups stand in a preferential position in relation to the government is to examine the degree to which business groups are involved in politics. The assumption behind this connection is that the more active the group is in politics, the greater its influence in government affairs which affect its or its members' interests.

Repeatedly during the interviews, I was told by group members that they considered the groups apolitical. The purpose of the group is to make money, not to win political power. Although the groups are not openly political, they do find it necessary to make campaign contributions, maintain personal relations with the party in power, and, through the individual political activities of one or another member of the group, assure themselves of some influence, no matter which government is in power. One interviewee described the situation as follows: "The groups do not openly admit their political activities, but they can exercise a critical weight in the political power balance when they chose to. " Another said, "Most groups work so as to not directly molest the government. They have good relations with the government underneath, although on the surface they may belong to different parties. "

The picture that emerges is one of entities too large and powerful not to play political roles in the country but which are primarily political in a defensive way. By and large, good treatment from the government is only a minor benefit of group membership, and most of the benefits come from the protection provided by the group against hostile action. This conclusion is, of course, limited to the two main groups in Nicaragua. It seems quite clear that the group associated with the ruling family is built around access to political power.

The fact that the fuling power in the country has its own distinct economic bloc not identified with the two groups studied may make Nicaragua unrepresentative of countries in which the political power is more diffused. It is difficult, however, to know whether this situation makes the groups more important to its members because it represents a counterweight to a highly concentrated political power, or whether the unusual situation makes the groups less important than they would normally be, because a number of the economic benefits normally captured by a business group are controlled by others.

Preferential Treatment by Nonmembers

Although a persuasive argument can be made that group membership results in a preferential status in the eyes of nonmembers, the Nicaraguan businessman by and large doubts the existence of such a preference and, if he believes it does exist, questions the idea that it converts into any economic benefit.

The argument maintains that people who are not members of the group, out of respect for the group or desire to incur its favor, will give members preferential treatment. They may sell group members goods at cheaper prices or on better terms, they may pay their bills more promptly or be inclined to extend credit more freely. They may also—other things being equal—purchase from a group-related firm, rather than from nongroup firms.

This type of advantage is not peculiar to the groups, but is the sort of advantage that the rich and the powerful have always enjoyed. Since most group members are rich and powerful in their own right, we have the same problem of showing both correlation and causality if we are to establish this preferential treatment as a function of group membership.

A very slight majority of the interviewees felt that a group firm receives preferential treatment from nongroup firms, but almost all agreed that this probably does not include prices, and several stressed the fact that in Nicaragua, personal relations, not group affiliations, determine preferences. *

When it came to measuring the value of this group service, almost all interviewees ranked it last. There is very little evidence that better treatment from nongroup members is a motivating factor in either forming or maintaining the group.

Operational Benefits

There are a number of ways in which the business group might contribute to a greater efficiency in a firm's operations. Economies of scale in the use of administrative and technical personnel, quick and reliable information, adversity insurance, and a means of solving the problem of succession are four potential examples of such services studied in Nicaragua.

------

*The interviewees were asked to compare the treatment which group firms A and B, a nongroup firm C, and a foreign firm D, would receive from an independent supplier. Table C.13 (in Appendix C) summarizes the question, answers, and comments.

Sixty percent of the interviewees indicated that membership in a group facilitates obtaining the services of specially-trained personnel in firm operations.* Nevertheless, the nearly total absence in practice of an interchange of personnel among the firms of the group (a pattern one would expect if economies of scale in the use of skilled personnel existed) tends to indicate the opposite. While there is some tendency for firms within a group to use the same lawyers, accountants, and consultants, many group members make it a policy to use different personnel for their personal businesses.

There are some signs which suggest that in the future groups may take advantage of this possibility. With the formation of holding companies, there is some talk of setting up a core of qualified executives to troubleshoot in the various firms of the group, but to date this can only be considered a very minor group function.

The groups have developed much further as an information network than as providers of technical and administrative support. A convincing majority of the interviewees felt that "information on the activities of the government or international economy which can effect my business reaches me much more rapidly through the group than other similar firms." Also, that "through my contacts in the group, I receive better information on markets and buyers, than other similar firms."

The business group also supplies a certain amount of adversity insurance. A member has a clear, if limited, duty to do what he can to help a fellow group member in trouble. † But this is a limited obligation; the group is primarily to "make money," while friends and family are for help in time of trouble. The response of one interviewee to a situation in which a fellow member was facing financial difficultues and needed a loan was:

> There is an obligation to learn of the matter in order to help, up to that point which my own judgement indicates. I would have to see real possibilities of success, before I would lend my personal money or that of the financial institution under circumstances such as you describe.

---

*Sixty-three percent of the interviewees felt that the following statement was true: "When I have a special project, it is possible to obtain from some firm or member of the group, trained personnel which would not be available to me if I were not a member of the group." Several of those who answered yes indicated that this already had occurred in one group but had not yet happened in another. Several interviewees, including one who answered that the statement was false, felt that this was not yet the pattern among the groups but was something they would do in the future.

†The obligation of help is revealed in the responses to a hypothetical situation of need in Table C.14 (in Appendix C).

The role of the business group in helping to solve the problem of succession, which often plagues the family firm, is still undefined. Although several interviewees claimed that groups help solve this problem, the groups are too young and the cases in which this problem has arisen within the group too few to indicate whether in fact this is the case. I doubt seriously that either the problem or the role of the group in dealing with it has received sufficient attention to make this potential group service a compelling reason for joining or staying in the group.

In summary, there is some evidence that groups provide certain operational services, as for example information, but by and large the group functions in this area are limited and the potential for operational benefits exceeds the reality. When the interviewees gave technical and administrative support a low ranking, they signalled the minor importance of these operational benefits in the formation and development of the groups.

Noneconomic Benefits

That the group has its social and psychological benefits is asserted by an overwhelming majority of group members. * The importance of these benefits varies, however, from person to person. The average group member tended to rank it third or fourth among the benefits of group membership, a ranking far greater than that given it by nongroup persons, who ranked it last (see Table C. 2, in Appendix C).

For most group members, the social status of group membership is relatively unimportant since family and economic position assure them the position they desire. The following remark of one interviewee was typical of most: "My social life is independent [of the group]; for me the reason for being in a group is to do business."

Nevertheless, many of them cited other members of the group whom they felt had joined the group primarily for the social status and personal contacts, since the economic benefits they derived from the group were insufficient to explain their behavior. Virtually all felt that their "respect from the business community and a position of leadership therein" was advanced by group membership.

The psychological benefits also rated high with most group members. Several stated that they felt one of the most important aspects, if not the most important, of group membership for them was the pleasure of working together for others. The rankings of their interview replies support these remarks, although the replies of those not in the groups express

_____

*Seventy percent of the interviewees considered that membership in a group has clear social and psychological advantages, as demonstrated in Table C. 15 (in Appendix C).

a certain cynicism about the importance of these motives when compared
to ones involving economic benefits.

I think, however, that the psychological benefits of group membership are more important than outsiders looking in generally assume.
True, the groups did not originally come together to fill psychological
needs, since they were primarily business arrangements. Nevertheless,
once established, the personal interactions within the board of directors, the sense of involvement in joint projects, and the feeling of sharing power and participating in important decisions are quite satisfying
to most of the members involved. After a time, these feelings could,
perhaps, become the most rewarding aspect of being in a group.

Some supporting evidence for this contention is the fact that both
group leaders noted that keeping a group together and maintaining a
united feeling was not easy. Each regularly devotes some of his time
to ensuring that the others feel involved. This is done by conferring
regularly with the various members and asking their advice. If psychological satisfaction were unimportant to group members, one would not
expect the "personal relations" or the "sense of involvement" to be so
important in keeping the group together as the leaders evidently consider
them to be.

In summary, the results of this research indicate that if the Nicaraguan business groups are representative, the business group functions
almost exclusively in the financial area, and that its principal importance is to facilitate credit to its members and help them make and manage their investments. Intragroup business and the insurance implicit
in any concentration of power are two other important, though lesser,
functions. Virtually all the rest are quite minor. These conclusions from
the 1971 study have been largely confirmed by events in the subsequent
years.

NOTES

1. M. Y. Yoshino, Japan's Managerial System: Tradition and Innovation (Cambridge, Mass.: M. I. T. Press, 1968), pp. 123, 129;
Joe S. Bain, International Differences in Industrial Structure: Eight
Nations in the 1950's (New Haven, Conn.: Yale University Press, 1966),
p. 87.

2. Simon Kuznets, Modern Economic Growth: Rate, Structure and
Spread (New Haven, Conn.: Yale University Press, 1966), pp. 1-26.

3. David Shelton, "The Banking System: Money and the Goal of
Growth, " in Public Policy and Private Enterprise in México, Raymond
Vernon, ed. (Cambridge, Mass.: Harvard University Press, 1964),
p. 210; Ricardo Lagos Escobar, La Concentración del Poder Económico:
Su Teoría, Realidad Chilena, 4th ed. (Santiago, Chile: Editorial del
Pacifico, 1962), pp. 161, 164; Chitoshi Yanaga, Big Business in Japan-
ese Politics (New Haven, Conn. and London: Yale University Press,
1968), p. 37.

4. Kozo Yamamuro, Economic Policy in Postwar Japan: Growth Versus Economic Democracy (Berkeley and Los Angeles: University of California Press, 1967), p. 112.

5. M. Y. Yoshino, Japan's Managerial System: Tradition and Innovation (Cambridge, Mass.: M. I. T. Press, 1968), p. 130.

6. Ibid., pp. 130, 139.

7. M. L. Kothari, Industrial Combinations: A Study of Managerial Integration in India Industries (Allahabad: Chaitanya Publishing House, 1967).

8. Dr. Raúl Hess, private interview held in San José, Costa Rica in early 1971.

9. R. K. Hazari, The Structure of the Corporate Private Sector: A Study of Concentration, Ownership and Control (London: Asia Publishing House, 1966), pp. 307, 308, 326-79.

10. Yoshino, op. cit., p. 131.

The first half of this chapter deals with some of the areas in which a knowledge of business group structure and behavior is likely to be a critical input to decision making and also some additional factors affecting the use of this knowledge in the decision-making process. In the second half, we turn our attention to the situation in which the manager must decide on whether to join or not join a business group. This topic provides a natural opportunity for a discussion of some of the costs of group membership.

THE GROUP FACTOR IN DECISION MAKING

The list of business decisions in which a knowledge of the structure and behavior of groups contributes to a better decision is enormous and limited only by our imaginative capacity to anticipate situations in which these large associations affect the ebb and flow of commerce. Nevertheless, if the picture of groups developed in the first four chapters is accurate, we should expect that these are the three areas in which the impact of group relations will be most critical: in financial decisions relating to credit and new investment opportunities; in marketing decisions in which the tradition of intragroup business and referrals affect buying decisions; and in decision making in which power or the ability to marshall pressure on others is critical, such as in dealings with the government or in all-out competitive struggles.

How the presence of business groups in the environment affects the decision will depend, of course, on the circumstances of the particular case and the position of the decision maker. There are no useful decision rules to aid the manager that I know of. The best advice for a manager in an environment of groups at this time is, "This is an important environmental element which could significantly affect the outcome of your activities. Know something about it, and keep it in mind as you analyze specific situations. " This sounds like an evasion of the question, but in fact in many areas of environmental analysis this simple, systematic common sense approach has proved the most useful.*

A concrete case is perhaps the best method of illustrating both the importance of the group factor and the type of analysis recommended. Imagine that a large multinational firm in oil and chemicals is contemplating a multimillion dollar investment in a nitrogen and fertilizer complex in the Philippines. At the time of the decision, say 1960 or thereabouts, there is no such plant in the country. To remedy this situation, the government, as part of its Five Year Development Plan, has given a privileged status to fertilizer projects. Local fertilizers are needed to substitute for imports and to supply a massive government drive to increase agricultural productivity.

The various projections of demand for nitrogen-based fertilizers during the coming five years range from 100, 000 to 400, 000 tons per year, depending largely on the optimism which the predictor has for the green revolution and the implementation of government plans. A review of these projections leads us to the conclusion that in the short run, even with government support, appreciable growth of fertilizer usage by the small highland farmers is not likely and that the bulk of the nitrogen will ultimately be used by the large, irrigated farms raising sugar and rice. Another potential customer is a steel mill which needs about 25, 000 tons of nitrogen a year.

Doubts about the size of demand are matched by uncertainties on the supply side. There are indications that five or six other firms are contemplating the same sort of investment even though it requires considerable capital. Among these are several multinational oil companies and three Philippine investors. The characteristics of the production process strongly recommend plants with a 60, 000 to 100, 000 ton per year capacity or greater. It is obvious, therefore, that even if the most optimistic forecast of demand proves correct, the market will not support the six or so plants contemplated.

To complete the picture, imagine a nascent nationalistic movement against foreign ownership of basic industry, a somewhat shaky government, and balance of payments problems. [1]

In this situation, I suspect most of us will conclude that the decision hangs on an analysis of how much of the nitrogen business of the

---

*At the Harvard Business School, the teaching materials and cases on Planning in the Business Environment demonstrate that in many of the complex areas of the environment, the most useful approach of the manager is precisely this simple, systematic, common sense approach. Models and decision-making rules of sufficient sophistication to be useful are generally unavailable for many of these important environmental factors. (See "Outline of a System of Concepts for Environmental Analysis and Corporate Planning, " Intercollegiate Case Clearing House, Harvard Business School.)

steel mill, the irrigated sugar and rice farms, and the government can
be captured, and what sort of arrangements (price or otherwise) will be
necessary to secure the business. This analysis, in turn, requires some
sort of predictions about how potential rivals will react to different situations. The idea of joint ventures or other cooperative arrangements
with the other oil firms and/or local investors will almost surely suggest
itself.

Now let us add an additional piece of information on group structure.
It turns out that the three potential builders of fertilizer plants belong
to the three most important business groups. Each group has its base of
influence with the government, although only one is publicly identified
with the current regime. In what way does this additional information
affect our calculations?

First, calculations of potential market share are bound to be altered
since it is now probable that the group-affiliated sugar and cotton plantations will give their business to affiliated firms and that only lower
prices are likely to woo them away. It is also likely that the local competitors will be able to offer severe competition for government business.
There is now even the possibility of a formidable coalition of business
groups with the nascent political movement against foreign firms.

Second, estimates of the financial capacity of the local investors
to mount their projects suddenly look better. They can almost surely
count on the support of local financial institutions and their backing in
the international capital markets.

Thirdly, our estimates of the responses of potential rivals must be
altered. Just as on an international level there is the phenomenon of the
defensive investment, so we can now expect that if one of the local
groups establishes its fertilizer plant, the others will be strongly tempted
to follow suit.

The specific case not only illustrates some of the many ways in
which a knowledge of the business groups may alter the process of decision making, but also provides a convenient framework for considering other factors affecting business group behavior. It is easy to become
slightly awed by the size of business groups and assume that an outsider up against the group is severely disadvantaged in securing credit,
capturing a share of the market or influencing the government. But group
power is not so overwhelming as it often appears on the surface. This
is because there are a number of pressures within and without the group
which tend to curb the impact of business groups, even in these areas
in which they are most active.

One of these factors is the tendency of power centers to stimulate
the formation of countervailing power centers. If there is a group pattern
of favoring fellow group members in business decisions, it is not unlikely that businessmen outside the group may follow a contrary policy.
If certain group farmers are most likely to discriminate in favor of their
group's fertilizer plant, it is also possible that the farmers associated
with different groups or unaffiliated with any group may prefer a neutral
supplier.

Knowing of this potential backlash movement, existing groups try not to let situations develop in which those outside the group feel compeled to form their own coalitions. Hence, there is a constant pressure checking the "preference for group members" principle.

Another set of factors mitigating the impact of groups on decision making might be labeled the centrifugal forces within the group. The diversity of interests and the fact that the components of the group have never achieved a complete community of interest means that there are strong internal pressures not to favor one part of the group at the expense of the other. This translates itself into a pattern of behavior in which buyers who are group members encourage outsiders to bid for their business.

It also leads them to avoid situations of complete dependence on a fellow group member. In the specific case above, it is likely that even if the steel mill belongs to a group which establishes its own nitrogen-producing plant, it will want to continue to buy a part of its needs from outside sources.

COSTS OF MEMBERSHIP IN A BUSINESS GROUP

A discussion of the different influences of the business group factor on specific decisions provides a good backdrop for considering the decision of a successful businessman who has just been invited to join one of the large business groups in his area.

This question when posed to a class of graduate students of Business Administration from several Latin American countries elicited the following response from one student: "Well, I guess the decision is obvious. I'd join. There are all sorts of economic advantages to being a member of the group and no disadvantages." Reflecting the same sort of judgment, close to 90 percent of the interviewees expressed the opinion that the successful businessman in today's Nicaragua is favorably disposed to joining a group if invited.

The behavior of a fairly sizeable number of Nicaraguan businessmen who remain independent or try to court both groups attests, however, to the fact that this decision to join is not an easy one.*

The reasons or advantages for joining a business group have already been dealt with at length in Chapter 4. They consist primarily of preferential access to credit and investment opportunities, intragroup business, protection and other benefits of concentrated economic power, and, to a lesser extent, administrative and technical support and other social benefits.

---

*In Nicaragua, the most notable example of a successful businessman who has been able to integrate himself with both groups is Manuel I. Lacayo. For a description of his activities, see Chapter 2, pp. 13 ff.

Arrayed against these benefits of group participation are the costs of group membership. Several of these costs have been touched indirectly in the previous section. First, it is possible that the preference given by certain firms is counterbalanced by the discrimination generated in others.

A second cost is the loss of independence; joining a group means giving up a certain degree of personal freedom of action. The other side of being able to call on a group member for help in time of need means being obligated to help in his time of need. The opportunity to share the investment opportunity of another means sharing your investment opportunities.

Finally, like all other large associations, business groups have costs of organization which probably increase with size. These costs, of communication and administrative coordination, for example, ultimately reduce the benefits which are available for distribution among the members.

It is not surprising, given this situation of both costs and benefits, that a number of businessmen have opted for a strategy of working with both groups, of trying to obtain the advantages of membership in both groups without the costs. Given the nature of the process by which groups court new members, this is a viable strategy for at least a certain amount of time. Sooner or later, however, I suspect that the businessman, like the coquette, tends to be forced to chose one suitor or the other, or neither.

NOTE

1. This example is a brief synopsis (with literary liberties) of "Multinational Oil Corporation (A), EA-R 444," a case of the Harvard Business School. I understand from a discussion with a case-writer involved in preparing this case that it also takes poetic license in disguising and structuring the real case on which it is based. The multinational oil corporation appears under the name of Mammoth Oil Company in the Promance Fertilizer Project case appearing in Paul W. Cook, Jr. and George A. Van Peterfy, Problems of Corporate Power (Homewood, Ill.: Richard D. Irwin, Inc., 1966).

CHAPTER

6

IMPACT ON
ECONOMIC DEVELOPMENT

The focus in this chapter is on the following question: "What impact, if any, do business groups have on the economic development of a country?" One way of beginning the discussion is by correlating the existence of business groups in a country with its rate of economic development. A quick review of Chapter 2 will demonstrate that several of the countries with the most heartening rates of economic growth in this century, such as Japan and México, are bastions of business groups. Unfortunately, so are countries like India, Chile, and Argentina which have not fulfilled their promise of growth.

Such a beginning to the discussion, however, would be misleading. Indirectly, it suggests that the group's impact on development is of great magnitude and measurable by reference to overall results, two very dubious propositions.* The first part of this chapter, therefore, is dedicated to placing the subject matter in perspective. The sections which follow discuss the various arguments which have led me to the concluding opinion that the net contribution of business groups to a country's development is beneficial during the initial period of the group's growth, but that at later stages the net contribution is probably unfavorable.

The title of this study is not meant to suggest that business groups are either the main stimulants of growth or, on the other hand, that they

---

*Even if we assume that future research confirms the hypothesis that business groups are a phenomenon regularly found in capitalist countries in the process of developing modern financial and industrial sectors, as we suggest at the end of Chapter 3, a moment's reflection will show that this does not imply that groups facilitate economic growth or even are a necessary part of it. To use an analogy, the almost perfect correlation between the appearance of cathouses and saloons with the beginnings of an economic boom in town does not imply that such enterprises are a contributing factor to growth.

poison or stunt it. The size of these groups and the activities they are engaged in make them important elements in their countries, but like most other aspects of developing societies, the business group is only part of a very complex, interdependent system. It may not even be the part of the system that merits the principal attention of theoreticians of economic development. The following hypothetical case underscores this need for a sense of perspective and at the same time introduces us to some of the difficulties of answering the question posed.

Suppose the government of a small country decides to stimulate development through a policy of encouraging import substitutions of certain industrial products. It does this by making investments in these industries very attractive. It offers subsidies of credit, high tariff barriers against the competition and tax exemptions, and other inducements. Imagine that Group X responds rapidly and establishes a small, relatively efficient plant. Group X's firm is quite profitable, but it turns out that the markets are so small and the uncontrollable costs so high that the firm will never reach a size at which it can sell at prices competitive with those in the world markets. The governmental economists come to the conclusion that they have foolishly nurtured the growth of uneconomical industries to the detriment of the country. The government has lost revenue; the consumers have paid high prices, and the capital has not gone to other areas with a higher developmental effect. At this point, we ask, "What is the impact of groups on economic development?"

"Harmful," replies one government economist. "Their success is a mirage, their wealth obtained at the expense of the government and the people, their contribution to growth minimal!" In a flush of rhetoric, he adds, "Abolish them!"

Is he correct? Perhaps in a certain sense, yes. In this case, the effects of group activity can be viewed as bad (detrimental to the total social welfare). Nevertheless, it seems clearly fallacious to ask that groups be abolished for responding so rapidly and effectively to the government's policies. Organizational arrangements this effective might be useful and indeed essential to rapid growth with proper government policies.

Complicate the example. Imagine that when the government decides to switch policies and reduce tariffs, the group mobilizes the industrial sector to protest such an action. Or, imagine that the industrialization policy is ultimately successful, in that an industry takes root in the country capable of competing in international markets, but that this occurs only after many years of subsidy by the government and the consumers.

As this single hypothetical example makes clear, any overall assessment of the impact of groups on economic development faces some formidable obstacles. First, the effects of the groups—not only the direct effects but the second, third, and fourth round effects—must be identified. A great unscrambling of the egg must take place. Second, these effects must be evaluated. Who or what gets credit for this or that result? With what do you compare the results? What might have happened had there been no groups? How do you determine what might have been?

Even if we can do all this, however, we are not home, for finally a value must be placed on the results. Since it is almost a certainty that some effects of the same act will be seen as valuable and others as not, what weights are assigned to the various results? How much "income distribution" do we give up for some "capital accumulation?" How much "market concentration" is "efficiency" worth?

It would be misleading to assume that the conclusion reached is the result of a process which has successfully surmounted these hurdles. Instead, my conclusions and the evidence which led me to them should be taken as opening remarks in a discussion of a question which is too important to avoid, even if it is too complicated to answer easily.

THE NEUTRAL TOOL THEORY

In a discussion of the role of business groups in economic development, one legitimate position is to argue that groups are essentially a neutral tool, an organizational arrangement which boosts or blocks development depending on whether its leaders are dynamic and progressive, or reactionary and conservative.

Such an argument is based on two observations. First, it is apparent that one of the most immediate results of the presence of groups within a country is their impact on the distribution of economic power. The pyramiding of companies and the interrelations among important firms in key sectors all lead to the concentration of important business decisions and powers in the hands of a relatively small number of men.

Second, it is obvious that the business group as an organizational arrangement is in many ways a tool. It is a tool used by the businessmen who are its members to achieve certain of their objectives, be they financial or marketing. It is also a tool which may conceivably be used by government policy makers as our hypothetical case illustrates. Because of the group's size, it is a powerful tool.

A powerful tool, the argument continues, is neither good nor bad. In the hands of progressive, socially-conscious businessmen, groups can lead the entire society towards a better world. In the hands of a decadent elite, they will be used for exploitation.

I have heard the difference between the Japanese experience and that of certain Latin American countries explained in precisely this way. The hardworking business elite who shaped the zaibatsu were driven by a great vision. They were seeking national independence and strength, the most rapid road to industrialization, and a place in the sun for all the Japanese people. While it is true that great family fortunes were the result of their activities, the stewards of these fortunes plowed them back into the economy; they did not squander them on conspicuous consumption or funnel them abroad to Swiss bank accounts. In short, the concentrated power and capital of the zaibatsu made a positive contribution to Japan's enviable growth rate.

The conclusion of this line of reasoning is that if the elite of certain Latin American countries have failed to use groups to lead their peoples to a higher growth rate, if they have squandered their power or used it timidly to reinforce their position of privilege in the society, this reflects on them as people—not on business groups as an organizational arrangement.

This neutral tool theory finds at least indirect support in the Central American experience. In countries like Costa Rica and Guatemala, more than in Nicaragua, public opinion divides the business groups into the "old" groups, groups founded on agricultural wealth and long-established businesses, and the "new" groups, associations formed in relatively recent times from the new industrial, construction, and agricultural businesses. It identifies "conservative" groups who seem wedded to traditional patterns and "modern" groups which exploit the new technologies and progressive business techniques. Although there are still some gaps to fill before "new" and "modern" groups are declared contributors to economic development, the beginnings of such an argument are easy to see.

There is undoubtedly some truth in the "neutral tool" theory and it serves to alert us to the possibility that there may be no generalization which can be applied uniformly to all business groups. I think, however, that the temptation of closing the discussion on this note must be resisted. The difficulty of an evaluation of groups which focuses on the personalities of the group members is that it fails to recognize the independent impact of differing organizational arrangements. Tools may be neutral in some moral sense, but rarely in the pragmatic realm. When political scientists discuss the merits and demerits of differing forms of political organization, when business administrators discuss the pros and cons of centralized versus decentralized decision making, they do so on the assumption that each organizational arrangement has built-in tendencies and characteristics which in the short or long run bear their own fruit, irrespective of the men in the organization.

THE PLUSES AND MINUSES APPROACH

A second approach to the impact of business groups on economic development is to select out a limited number of factors that are believed to play a critical role in economic development and examine the impact of business groups on each of these. Although incomplete, this approach has the advantage of reducing the task to a more manageable level.

Three factors have been regarded by students of economic development as having critical importance: capital formation, entrepreneurial innovation, and social development. We examine the impact of business groups on each of these in the sections which follow.

Capital Formation and Allocation

Arthur Lewis in his classic work The Theory of Economic Development stressed that one of the critical determinants of economic growth is the rate of capital formation:

> [C]ommunities in which the national income per head is not increasing, invest 4 or 5 percent of their national income per annum or less, whilst progressive economies invest 12 percent per annum or more. The central problem in the theory of economic growth is to understand the process by which a community is converted from being a 5 percent to a 12 percent saver—with all the changes in attitudes, in institutions, and in techniques which accompany this conversion. [1]

How do the groups which are themselves a species of financial intermediary and also centers of wealth affect the rate of capital formation within the developing country and the efficiency with which it is allocated?

It is hard to believe that business groups directly affect the overall savings rate within a country. There is little evidence that I know of in Nicaragua which would indicate that group members as individuals differ in their consumption habits from their nonmember counterparts. While it is probable that group firms have a higher reinvestment rate than nongroup firms, this is probably due to the fact that their firms are growing more rapidly and, therefore, in need of more capital.

The majority of interviewees did not believe that group members are less likely to invest part of their money abroad, although several individuals did express the strong opinion that, by and large, group members have greater faith in the future of the country and are, as a consequence, reinvesting a greater percentage of their savings locally than nongroup members.

Indirectly, the groups have probably contributed to a rise in the overall savings rate by the role they have played in the development of the financial sector. There is little doubt that the saver in Nicaragua in 1976 finds a much more attractive menu of financial assets from which to chose than he did in 1960. There are savings accounts in national and private banks paying 6 percent, and bonds and notes paying 8 to 10 percent. Accompanying the greater diversity of offerings offered since

1960 has been a notable increase in the Nicaraguan financial system, [2] and if official statistics are accurate, an increase in the private savings rate from 12 percent in 1960 to 16 percent in 1970. [3] It is unlikely that the financial sector would have developed as rapidly as it has or that rates paid to savers would be as high as they are without the activity of the groups.

The impact of business groups on the efficiency of capital allocation is probably more significant than their role in capital formation. It is also more interesting. Two contrary arguments can be made. It can be argued that group firms tend to monopolize the sources of financing and, by giving preferential financing to members, encourage investments within the group that have a lower rate of return than investments that would be made by nongroup members.

The argument spelled out goes as follows. The study of business groups in Nicaragua revealed that the two major business groups control over 70 percent of the total assets of the private financial sector, which is eloquent evidence to their control of the allocation of the savings (national and international) that flow through the financial institutions. The study of the business groups also revealed the clear belief within the Nicaraguan business community that members of the business groups receive preferential access to this credit. It is thus probable that when a member and nonmember both have projects, and capital is scarce, the member gets the credit even when his project has a lower rate of return (after adjustment for risk) than the nonmember's project. As a result, the country loses the greater return which the nonmember's project would have provided.

There are several factors which greatly weaken this argument. First, to be valid, this argument requires that interest rates be the final allocators of credit. In fact, the interest rates charged to borrowers by the banking system are regulated by the Central Bank and generally do not adequately reflect the demand for credit. Also, in their credit allocation, groups generally do not give their members preference in regard to interest rates. Thus, even if a preference exists, it does not necessarily lead to investments with a lower rate of return.

Second, the argument is build around a model of capital allocation which has a certain air of unreality to it. In Nicaragua, at least, almost all projects come to bankers showing returns considerably in excess of the cost of capital, a return in no way dependent on a difference of one or two points in the interest rate. The banker will probably discount these returns by a significant factor to make allowance for unexpected events which are likely to arise. But since neither he nor the investors know with any sense of certainty what the return is likely to be, the loan is rarely, if ever, denied or granted on the basis of the projections.

The contrary argument makes the point that, in their environment, business groups tend to represent a step toward, rather than away from, more efficient and rational allocation of capital. First, in creating financial intermediaries which have the confidence of the public, they create an instrument that can move savings from low-yield areas such as land to higher-yield investments in industry, thus increasing the rate of return.

By institutionalizing the credit allocation function and managing it within the groups, they can exercise pressure to see that the capital yields a higher rate of return. As most persons working in the financial institutions will tell you, the banker's big job is not just to spot the more profitable investment (as if somehow investments are on a pre-ordained course to success or failure) but often to intervene to ensure that the firm achieves those profits. * By reducing the real and perceived risks to capital transfers, the business groups reduce the risk premium required by the lender and thus facilitate a greater capital flow.

My own evaluation of these two arguments is that at least in the early stages of development, the average business group makes a positive contribution to both capital mobilization and allocative efficiency. Business groups may not be the optimal or most efficient financial intermediaries in all types of environment, but they are one of the most efficient and viable intermediaries in an underdeveloped environment.

Innovation and Entrepreneurship

Joseph Schumpeter in his tremendously important work Capitalism, Socialism, and Democracy focused the attention of the world's economists on the role of the innovator and the entrepreneurs, which in his view was "to reform or revolutionize the pattern of production by exploiting an invention or, more generally, an intried technological possibility for producing a new commodity or producing an old one in a new way, by opening up a new source of supply of materials or a new outlet for productions, by reorganizing an industry and so on."[4] This role is critical in the development process; the success of the capitalist engine in producing growth is tied to people who perform this creative entrepreneurial function "of getting things done."

How well do groups innovate? Are they dynamic pioneers in new fields, or are they cautious and conservative? Do they support the elements for change in the business community, or do they try to squash the new entrepreneurs? Are they good administrators?

---

*There is a complicated but beautiful case which may illustrate this point. In Nicaragua a private financiera was set up to channel AID loan funds to the private sector and into new investments. Like many other financieras of this kind, it has run into difficulties which, according to at least several persons who know the situation well, stem not so much from a faulty as from weak administration of these projects once they were established.

Once again it is possible to take a position on either side of this question. One can argue that groups are conservative, a part of the reactionary establishment. Or one can claim, on the other hand, that they represent the dynamic and the aggressive tendencies in the business community and that they are leading the way toward professionalism and rationality in the practice of business.

In general, the evidence in Nicaragua suggests that the business groups are among the most aggressive entrepreneurs and the most professional managers in the society. One bit of evidence is their rapid growth during the past 15 years and the role played by groups in many of the newly-established firms. A second is the professional esteem in which they are held by the rest of the business community. When the interviewees were asked to compare the quality of professional people working with the groups with those working with nongroup firms and foreign firms, those in and out of the group ranked group executives with the highest ratings. A third piece of evidence is the way in which the business groups in Central America have been leaders in hiring M. B. A. graduates and emphasizing professional management practices.

Group behavior in this respect is probably not accidental. There are structural pressures within the group to better performance, which give it a more modern or innovative bias than the traditional family firms. The leaders are aware that the ties binding the disparate elements together are economic and that profitability is essential to survival.

In comparison with their peers, group members are quite modern and progressive. Nevertheless, in Nicaragua, it is not so clear that they have been more innovative than the national development bank, INFONAC, or other government-sponsored agencies. Nor is it clear that they have been progressive and innovative enough to bring Nicaragua to that level of full employment which is necessary if the country is to enjoy a long-term stability and prosperity. *

It should also be noted that there are several long-range aspects of group development which make it probable that the older, more mature groups contribute less in the way of innovation and pioneering leadership than the younger groups.

In the formative years, the group is climbing to a position of power. Its growth will almost always depend upon its being situated in a number of fast-growing, profitable industries. The groups, in other words, achieve an initial critical mass from firms who have successfully adapted new technology to old activities or who are leaders in developing new industries. Having reached a position of relatively great size, the

---

*There are no reliable unemployment statistics in Nicaragua, much less projections of future unemployment. In a neighboring country, Costa Rica, however, the Minister of Labor recently told a gathering of businessmen that the private sector was generating less than 15 percent of the jobs required to absorb the population entering the job market.

job of maintaining historic growth rates becomes increasingly difficult.
About this time an alternative business strategy opens up. The concentration of power within the group makes the elimination of competition
and the use of political power an increasingly feasible road to profits.
I suspect that the great majority of business groups find this temptation
difficult to resist and, in their more mature years, follows a strategy
built more on power than on performance, a strategy whose contribution
to development and general welfare is much smaller.

Social Development

Finally, economists and others are almost universally agreed that
in measuring and defining development, the noneconomic results must
be included. This, in part, reflects value systems which insist that
development is only significant if it means more than GNP, that, for
example, equality in the distribution of the benefits of increased production is as important as an increase in the total output.

Groups undoubtedly lead to a concentration of economic power and
the economic benefits of that power. The resulting inequities, then,
must be viewed as a negative contribution to be weighed against the
positive economic functions performed by the group.

A preoccupation with social factors is more than a statement of personal values. It also reflects an awareness that what is often considered noneconomic—human development and social institutions—cannot be
separated from what is considered economic. For example, it is likely
that distribution of income directly affects the levels of nutrition, education, and self-respect of the populace, which, in turn, directly affect
productivity. Similarly, it is not unreasonable to believe that a distribution of political power develops a sense of responsibility and capacity
in those who have it, which, in turn, creates the social cohesion and
discipline a nation needs for its march forward. It is hard to establish
and measure the impact that the groups have on development in this manner, but insofar as they participate in and contribute to an unbalanced
distribution of wealth and power, it is probably negative.

Where does this leave us? In summary I would argue that groups
tend to be a valuable transitional organization form for societies starting
on the road of industrialization. They perform important financial services effectively. They are generally innovative and aggressive in the
pursuit of production techniques and opportunities. As the adjective
"transitional" implies, however, there comes a time when the contributions of these associations are not as important or as pronounced as
they once were, and then the undesirable concentration of power and
costs they engender outweigh the positive contributions.

I would also suggest that since much of business group behavior
is a strategic response to environmental conditions, perhaps as impor-

tant a question as whether or not business groups contribute to development is the question of what sort of governmental policies tend to encourage socially useful business group behavior and to minimize less desirable group behavior.

This conclusion underscores the need for more studies which throw light on the inner dynamics of business groups. It is especially important to begin to break ground in the analysis of how groups respond to different governmental policies and environmental conditions. Historical studies, detailed case studies, and cross-cultural comparisons can all provide information, but for these to be truely useful a standard terminology must be developed, and field descriptions must be accompanied by attempts to create explanatory models.

It is my belief that an effort to broaden our knowledge of family and business groups will be useful to a variety of decision and policy makers in both the private and public sectors. It also will indirectly help to reveal many of the environmental conditions in the developing world that discourage productive practices. More complete knowledge of groups may even help us in the elusive search for ways of turning certain traditional family and cultural patterns of the developing world from liabilities into assets in the modernization process.

NOTES

1. W. Arthur Lewis, The Theory of Economic Growth (Homewood, Ill.: Richard D. Irwin, Inc., 1955), pp. 225-26.

2. A measure of this growth is the relation of financial assets flowing through the financial system to the GNP, which increased from 25 percent in 1960 to 47 percent in 1970. (Banco Central de Nicaragua, Informe Anual, 1970, pp. 38, 39, 62.)

3. Ibid., p. 72.

4. Joseph A. Schumpeter, Capitalism, Socialism, and Democracy, 3rd ed. (New York: Harper & Brothers, 1942), p. 132.

APPENDIX A:
FIELD WORK AND
METHODOLOGY

The main sources of information in this book are the results of lengthy interviews of a group of approximately 40 Nicaraguans, held in early 1971. Approximately 15 of these subjects completed followup interviews in the summer of 1975. This interview information is supplemented by approximately 80 written questionnaires completed in the summer of 1971, and by government surveys, statistical reports, financial statements, and reports on specific events. The period of research from 1970 to 1975 covers the time during which I have lived in Nicaragua and been a member of the faculty of the Instituto Centroamericano de Administración de Empresas.

THE INTERVIEW SAMPLE

A sample of approximately 50 people was selected for detailed interviews in 1971, after a period of preliminary investigation. These people were chosen from a list of names of over 200 people which the researcher had collected during the preliminary period. Inclusion on the original list was based on either a group affiliation (known or suspected) prominence in the business community of Nicaragua, or a good knowledge of business community.

The original sample of 50 was composed of 15 people from each of the two major groups and 20 who were not affiliated with either group. Those from each group included full-time, top-level executives, major shareholders, directors of group firms, and several persons with special relations to the group. The nongroup interviewees included businessmen, successful and important members of several of the smaller groups, economists, government officials, a reporter, and several executives of U. S. subsidiaries.

The interviewees were not chosen at random. Candidates were selected to ensure that the sample included people representing different positions within and without the groups. Another criterion was that the candidates be articulate and candid. Since I only knew personally three or four of the people at the beginning of the interviews, I relied on colleagues and close friends for help in selecting the sample. During the process of interviewing, three people were added to the sample list at the recommendation of the people being interviewed. Thirty-nine people were actually interviewed although not all of them completed each part of the interview. Table A. 1 describes by group affiliation those of the sample list who completed the interview.

TABLE A. 1

Interview Sample

Affiliation	Actually Interviewed	Sample Chosen*
Banco de América Group	11	16
Banco Nicaraguense Group	12	17
Other	16	20
Smaller groups	5	6
Government and government agencies	5	5
Nongroups and nongovernment	6	9
Total	39	53

*With three additions made during the period of interviewing.
Source: Compiled by the author.

The group affiliation of the interviewee was derived from his own description of himself and how he was classified by the other persons interviewed.

The role a group member plays within his group varies. Some are primarily shareholders, others directors and shareholders, others full-time executives, and others consultants or trusted advisors. Table A. 2 describes the people interviewed by the main role which they play within the group-owned businesses. A man's role within the group-owned businesses is not necessarily the same as his principal career role; many of the directors of group-owned businesses are fulltime executives of their own businesses.

Virtually all of the people interviewed were men of business, that is, men who have dedicated time during their careers to the administration of firms, the handling of business affairs, and the making of money. A great many, however, also had professional training, as Table A. 3 demonstrates.

Considering the general level of professional training of the businessmen of Nicaragua, the sample is clearly skewed toward those who are sophisticated and educated. Three factors appear to contribute to this skewedness. In Nicaragua, professional education is an important criterion for chosing men for leadership positions in the government and business, and leaders were deliberately chosen for the sample. Most of the group members come from the upper-middle and higher classes and therefore generally have enjoyed the advantages of higher education. Finally, the men who were recommended as articulate may have been thought of as articulate because of their education.

Table A. 4 describes the sample by approximate age. The relative youthfulness of the leading businessmen and top government officials of Nicaragua was something of a surprise, and was related in great part to their professional training.

TABLE A. 2

Interviewees' Roles Within the Group

Role	Banco de América	Banco Nicaraguense	Total
Shareholder-Director	5	7	12
Full-time executive of group-owned firms	4	3	7
Special	2	2	4
Total	11	12	23

Source: Compiled by the author.

TABLE A. 3

Professional Training of Interview Sample

Training	Number
Business Administration[a]	9
Engineers or Architects	8
Lawyers[b]	10
Economists[b]	7

[a]One interviewee had professional degrees in both law and business administration.
[b]Three interviewees had professional degrees in both law and economics.
Source: Compiled by the author.

TABLE A. 4

Estimated Age of Interview Sample

Age	Number
Under 30	3
30-50	25
50 or above	11

Source: Compiled by the author.

What does the sample represent? There are probably 30 to 50 people who would be considered members of each of the two major groups.
A number of these would be marginal or not very important members.
There are probably from three to eight key members in each group, and
perhaps 20 full members. If this estimate of the size of the group is
accurate, then the people in the interview probably represent 50 percent
of the key members, 35 percent of the full members, and 25 percent of
all members of the two major groups. The people in the "Other" category
represent much larger populations. Virtually all of the smaller independent groups are represented in the sample.

The people interviewed were not selected to represent any single
set of opinions. They were chosen to represent different viewpoints
within and without the groups. The viewpoints represented in the sample
include those of young, well-educated, ambitious executives who are,
in a sense, the technicians of the groups, those of the successful businessmen who have accumulated or administer a sizable estate, and those
of the government officials concerned with formulating and implementing
economic policy for the nation.

The similarity of opinions of those with distinct roles was somewhat
surprising. Although the replies were all tabulated to reveal differences
of opinion between subsets of the sample, these differences by and large
failed to materialize. For example, the responses of the government
economists in the sample were not noticeably different from those of the
wealthier group members who serve only as directors. The similarity of
responses is evidence that the interview results reflect the opinions in
Nicaragua of the big businesses and of the politicians in the major parties. The sample is sufficiently large to ensure that the opinions sought,
namely beliefs of Nicaraguan businessmen on the advantages of group
membership, are reflected with fair accuracy. The results do not necessarily reflect the opinions of the very small businessman, in so far as
he has opinions on the subjects of this study, or the opinions of university students, or the more radical political parties, or of other interest groups such as the Church.

The absence of the replies of 11 persons who were selected for interviewing but were not interviewed should not bias the results. The
principal reason these people were not interviewed was the difficulty
of arranging the interview. The people chosen for interviewing represented the wealthiest and most active businessmen and highest-ranking
government officials in Nicaragua, and some could not afford the time
for a two to four and one-half hour interview. Another reason stemmed
from the sensitive nature of the subject, which caused several people
to indicate that they preferred not to participate. The 11 included a
disproportionate number of the older, wealthy businessmen and, unfortunately, reduced the representation of this group in the interview
sample.

In spite of the time demanded and the sensitive nature of the information requested, the vast majority of the interviewees cooperated with

a willingness and candor far greater than I expected. There were a number of reasons for this cooperation, including: the Latin tradition of courtesy; the introductions which several close friends gave me; and the prestige and respect which INCAE has with the business community of Nicaragua. It is also possible that because the political atmosphere in Nicaragua is unusually conservative when compared with other places in Latin America, the groups have not yet felt pressured to adopt a low-profile strategy, which would have made data-gathering on the groups difficult.

THE INTERVIEW

The interview took from two to four and one-half hours, and averaged over three hours. A complete interview consisted of:

1. The construction of a verbal definition of the group.

2. The classification of approximately 90 well-known people in Nicaragua by group affiliation.

3. The classification of approximately 54 business firms by group affiliation.

4. Background information on the interviewee, and his relation to the group, group operations, and decision making.

5. An evaluation and ranking by the interviewee of certain possible advantages of group membership.

6. The opportunity to answer questions and make comments on group-related topics such as family, caudillo, public opinion, impact on development, and likely future developments of the groups.

Not every part of the interview was appropriate to each interviewee. There were also cases where the interviewee could not dispose of sufficient time for a complete interview, and so completed those sections in which I believed his replies would be most helpful.

The number of respondents for each of the six sections is given in Table A.5. There were some questions within each of these sections which not everyone answered. There were also some questions in which the reply was "don't know" and which, therefore, was not included in the tabulated results. When the reply was conditional or different from the suggested alternatives, these were recorded either as "clarifying" comments or as "special" answers and were included in the tabulated results.

The interview was conducted from a written set of questions. Interview questions went through two basic revisions. The original set of questions was revised in the light of comments by faculty advisors. It was then administered to a few of the interviewees. A second revision was made after the first set of interviews, and after some additional recommendations by faculty advisors. During the course of interviewing, several new questions were introduced into the questionnaire.

TABLE A. 5

Respondents to Different Sections of the Interview,
by Group Affiliation

| Section | Group Affiliation | | | |
	Banco de América	Banco Nicaraguense	Other	Total
Verbal definition	10	10	13	33
Classification of 90 well-known businessmen	10	11	14	35
Classification of 54 business firms	8	6	12	25
Evaluation of advantages of group membership	10	10	14	35
Background information	—	—	—	30
Additional comments and opinions	—	—	—	30

Source: Compiled by the author.

Also, approximately half way through the interviews, the random order of potential advantages in the lists requiring ranking was rearranged randomly to reduce bias of order in the answers.

The source for the list of 90 persons to be classified was a larger list of 200 names, which I had compiled during preliminary investigations. Names of potential group members were taken from the boards of directors of those firms believed to be part of the group. Prominent businessmen were taken from a list of supporters of INCAE, while the names of prominent government officials, economists, and business consultants were given to me by colleagues and friends. This larger list was reduced to 90 names for the classification section of the interview. Several criteria governed the choice of the 90 names. The people on the list had to be well known. The list had to include as many different types of group members as possible. The list had to include not only "clear examples" of the different types of people in a group but also "difficult" cases. The number of names chosen by following this criteria came to 75. Another 15 randomly chosen names were added to the list and all of the names were arranged in alphabetical order.

The list of 54 firms was compiled in a similar manner. The basic objective was to present the interviewees with a list of well-known firms from the different sectors of the economy. The firms were arranged on the list by sector and alphabetically within each sector.

I administered all the interviews and generally recorded the answers. Comments explaining the answers were noted and in cases where the reply was unexpected or unusual, I often asked the interviewee to explain his answer. I then recorded his comments as close to verbatim as possible. When concrete examples or specific illustrations were given as part of an answer, these were recorded. The interviewee was often asked to elaborate on them. The interviewee was also given an opportunity to make open-ended observations on the groups both at the beginning and at the end of the interview. In addition, he was asked to indicate how comfortable he felt with the alternatives being given him for his answers on certain of the questions. Virtually all of the people interviewed indicated that they understood the questions, and that in their opinion, the questions were focused on the important aspects of the group.

Many of the people interviewed became my social friends and in several cases at parties or later encounters would add to their remarks or give additional information. These I recorded in memoranda for my records, along with miscellaneous information and clippings on the groups, which I have collected during the course of my five years in Nicaragua. Where this information appeared relevant to explain, contradict or throw some light on the more formally-gathered information, it has been included. It goes without saying that I am in debt for many of my generalizations and opinions to these discussions with friends, even in cases in which I cannot acknowledge the debt.

THE QUESTIONNAIRES

In June, when most of the interviews had been completed, a written questionnaire was prepared and administered to all the graduate students of business at INCAE. The student body of INCAE at that time consisted of 110 graduate students of business administration from all the Central American countries, and from Panamá, Colombia, Ecuador, and Perú. The median age of the students was 26; the great majority had already had experience in business. Many of them came to INCAE from executive positions and most planned to return to work in business.

The questionnaires were completed as part of the assignments for a class entitled "Groups, Their Impact on Decision Making and Economic Development," which was given to both the first and second year classes. I conducted the class and after class collected all those questionnaires which students were willing to have used in this research. A total of 61 students turned in their questionnaires. In addition, shortly after class, I made detailed notes on the comments and discussion of the class period.

The same procedure was followed in the Advanced Management Program held in Managua in July of 1971. Thirty-nine participants attended the program, representing all of the countries of Central America, and Panamá. The majority were from 30 to 45 years of age and came from executive positions for a six-week course. Nineteen turned in their questionnaires for use in this study. Table A.6 gives the total response

TABLE A. 6

Sample of Students Who Completed Questionnaire,
by Country and Course

Country	2nd Year	1st Year	PAG*	Total
Nicaragua	15	15	9	39
Guatemala	4	1	1	6
El Salvador	6	1	1	8
Honduras	4	—	4	8
Costa Rica	1	6	1	8
Panamá	2	1	3	6
Colombia	2	3	—	5
Ecuador	—	1	—	1
Perú	1	—	—	1
Total	35	28	19	82

*Participants of Advanced Management Course at INCAE.
Source: Compiled by the author.

by country and by class. On the average, more than half of the students
turned in their questionnaires.

The students and executives represent a different group than most
of the people interviewed. They are young professionals, many of whom
come from the middle class. The students also tended to be considerably
more liberal in their political opinions than the average businessman.
Their answers, nevertheless, seem to parallel closely those of the interviewees, even in those answers which reflect favorably on the groups.

BIAS

The interview questions forced many of the interviewees to consider
the group more analytically than they ever had previously. Several said
they were stimulated to think about possible advantages of group membership, and it is probable that certain advantages of membership were
suggested that some interviewees would not have thought of on their
own. This makes it important to distinguish to what degree the answers
reflect the interviewees' own opinions, and to what degree they reflect
what was "learned" in the interview itself.

The "learning" aspect of the interview was deliberate. For the interviews to yield a sophisticated evaluation of all the potential advantages of group membership and, ultimately, a ranking, it was important
that in the course of the interview a uniform terminology about groups

and their advantages develop. Similarly, each interviewee had to be encouraged to break down his general ideas into progressively more specific parts, and to analyze these. And it was also necessary to suggest certain potential advantages that he might not have considered so that he could express opinions on them.

This made it necessary to express ideas and opinions in some questions that could easily bias answers to other questions. Also, some of the ideas had to be worded in a persuasive manner, first as a way of articulating the idea more clearly and differentiating it in the interviewee's mind from related but distinct ideas, and secondly as a way of raising potentially sensitive subjects without scaring the interviewee into silence.

Although some of the wording leads to a potential biasing of the interview results, we can be reasonably certain that the major findings of the study were not affected by the bias introduced. There are several reasons for this.

First, the interview was arranged in such a manner that questions moved from general subjects carrying no bias to the more specific ones which by their wording or the ideas they suggested could have introduced bias. A comparison of the early answers with those later in the interview show that there was no significant shift of opinion among the interviewee

Second, the replies and rankings to the questionnaires, in which there was virtually no "conditioning," came out almost identical to those in the much longer personal interviews.

Third, in the use of the results in those sections of the interview where ideas were persuasively worded, little weight has been placed on the absolute answers, where the bias would show, and much more weight on the relative position of the answers, where presumably the bias is the same and cancels out.

Fourth, the interviewees, perhaps because of their professional training or high positions of responsibility, demonstrated a mental toughness which I had not expected. Few seemed to be swayed by the phrasing of the questions. It was my distinct impression that most of the interviewees were expressing their own opinions. Many, as they admitted, had never thought much about what the groups did or did not do because the groups had developed "naturally." When asked to weigh and analyze reasons, many went back into their experiences and organized them to bear on a question that they had not previously considered. Thus, the answers were their own; the learning came from having asked themselves new questions.

THE FOLLOWUP INTERVIEW

In 1975, 15 of the original interviewees were selected for followup interviews of approximately one to two hours. The followup sample was chosen from the original group of cooperative interviewees to represent the different major groups and subgroups.

The followup interview was designed to seek information on people who have joined or left the group, on new investment and businesses with each, and on the way in which each group has responded to certain external crises, such as the 1972 earthquake, or internal crises such as those provoked by the death of an important group member. One set of questions also focused on the groups' political activities in the 1974 election and their current relation to the government. Another set of questions dealt with changes in managerial style and processes within each group.

OTHER INFORMATION

In addition to the information gathered in the structured field work, I was able to talk about the groups with several important businessmen and economists in countries other than Nicaragua. These countries include Guatemala, Costa Rica, Panamá, Colombia (Bogotá and Medellín), and Venezuela (Caracas).

Most of the statistics were provided by the Banco Central, specifically the Department of Technological Studies and the Department of Economic Studies. I was able to make use of unpublished surveys of various sectors of Nicaragua, the latest revised GNP figures, and a "sources and uses" study prepared for the bank by Professor Nicolás Marín. By talking directly with the people who had prepared the numbers, I was able to gain considerable insight into the world they were trying to describe and some idea of the relative credibility of the numbers.

A plan to secure income and balance sheet statements from group firms (except where these were already public) was abandoned early in the research. As was mentioned earlier, the difficulty of securing accurate, comparable information on both group and nongroup firms discouraged any systematic and objective study on the performance of the groups. Some rough estimates of the profitability of group and nongroup firms prepared by Professor Marín for his thesis on industrial financing in Nicaragua are discussed in Chapter 4.

PRESENTATION OF RESULTS

Two types of numerical summaries of responses are used in this study. One is the percentage of a given reply. This is derived by dividing the number of similar replies by the total number of replies. In most tables, this percentage can be reconverted easily to the original number of responses by multiplying it by the number of respondents whose replies are included in the table.

Where it was possible to give more than a yes or no answer and where the answers could be arranged on a continuum (for example, "much more," "more," "same," "less," "much less"), the results were often summarized in an index. This index is nothing more than a weighted average of the replies, in which numerical equivalents on a continuum represent the verbal answers.

For several reasons, sophisticated statistical manipulations of most of the data gathered in the study were considered inappropriate. The subsamples, which are small, were not randomly chosen and most of the answers given do not pretend to a precision that would justify fine mathematical interpretations. Chi-square tests, however, were used to help determine whether in specific cases the responses of one subsample were significantly different from another; they rarely were. A chi-square test was also used as a means of dramatically illustrating the existence of a uniform perception of groups in Nicaragua.

Nicaragua[1] is a small Central American country located between
Honduras and El Salvador on the north, and Costa Rica on the south. It
is a typical Central American country (as typical as one of these unique
countries can be), and although small, it is representative in many ways
of the other Hispano-American countries. It is about the size of Penn-
sylvania, 45,000 square miles, but has only 2 million people, fewer
than either Pittsburgh or Philadelphia. [2]

Nicaragua would be classed as one of the world's less developed
countries. The average per capita income as can be seen in Table B.1
is $350, but even this meager income is not distributed evenly. Over
half of the population is illiterate, and less than 5 percent graduate
from high school. Infant mortality is high. [3] Nevertheless, according
to a World Bank survey, Nicaragua is blessed with natural resources
capable of sustaining a larger population at a higher standard of living.[4]

The Nicaraguan people are primarily mestizo (a mixture of the white
European immigrants and the native Indian population) and ladinos (of
Hispanic culture). Spanish is the official language; a civil law legal
system holds sway; approximately 96 percent of the people are Roman
Catholic. [5]

A person looking for evidence of Hispano-American personality and
cultural traits—the mañana syndrome, machismo, the cult of the caudillo,
a propensity to cultivate the arts and not the sciences—can easily find
them in Nicaragua, often reflected in business practices. None of this
is surprising in view of Nicaragua's history. Nicaragua was discovered
in 1522 by Gil González de Avila on an expedition of the Spanish crown,
was settled two years later by Spaniards under Pedrarias, Governor of
Panamá, and remained a Spanish colony for 300 years. [6] What is perhaps
surprising is the number of non-Spanish names one finds in any roster
of group members; a fact which reflects the not insignificant immigration
to Nicaragua since 1800 from Eastern and Western European countries
and England, and the positions of influence acquired by these immigrants.

Nicaraguan history has been marked from the beginning by corrupt
government, factionalism, civil wars, dictatorships, foreign intervention, and the exploitation of one part of the populace by another. Small
wonder, therefore, that a cohesive, cooperative society has been a long
time in coming and that the typical Nicaraguan businessman finds things
like relative power, security, and devices for stabilizing his environment of great importance.

The pattern was set quite early in the game. The conquest and exploitation of Nicaragua by the Spanish was rapid, brutal, and ultimately
wasteful. [7] Gold, the principal objective of first explorers, was taken
from the Indians. Then the Indians themselves were shipped out to Perú

TABLE B.1

Nicaragua's Population, GNP, and Foreign Trade

	Population (in thousands)	Total GNP (thousands of dollars in 1958)	GNP Per Capita (U.S. dollars)	Average Exports/ Imports Per Capita (U.S. dollars)
1500	1,000	—	—	—
1600	20	—	—	—
1700	150	—	—	—
1800	250	—	—	—
1900	402	—	—	—
1910	501	—	—	17.88
1920	634	—	—	23.52
1930	—	—	—	25.26
1940	830	—	—	23.32
1950	1,050	214,000	205	32.25
1960	1,411	341,800	242	40.40
1970	1,833	686,800	375	68.10
1974	2,083	869,400	417	100.90

Sources: Population: David R. Radell, Historical Geography of Western Nicaragua: The Spheres of Influence of Léon, Granada, and Managua, 1519-1965. Report on Field Work carried out under ONR Contract Nonr-3656(03), Project NR 388 067 (Department of Geography, University of California, Berkeley, James J. Parsons, Principal Investigator, 1969), p. 233, for 1500-1950; Dept. de Estudios Económicos, Banco Central de Nicaragua, Indicadores Económicos 1, no. 2 (July 1975) for 1960-74. GNP: Dept. de Estudios Económicos, Banco Central de Nicaragua, Indicadores Económicos 1, no. 2 (July 1975). Average Exports/Imports: Pedro Belli, "An Inquiry Concerning the Growth of Cotton Farming in Nicaragua" (Ph.D. diss., University of California, Berkeley, 1958), p. 50, for 1900-50; Dept. de Estudios Económicos, Banco Central de Nicarague, Indicadores Económicos 1, no. 2 (July 1975), for 1960-74.

as slaves.[8] The Indians were not the only ones to suffer from the corrupt and inefficient provincial government. Pedrarias and his two successors Francisco Castañeda and Rodrigo de Contreras so openly engaged in the illegal confiscation of encomiendas (grants of territory and tribute-paying Indians) that, in 1548, the power to grant them was moved from León to Guatemala.[9]

Corruption also had an immediate and negative impact on the development of local industries. During the sixteenth century, for example, a shipbuilding industry was begun on the Pacific port of Realejo. While shipbuilding continued here during the next two centuries, ultimately Realejo, in spite of some excellent natural comparative advantages, lost out in competition to the Philippines due "to government corruption, administration inefficiency, the abuse of labor, climate, and pirates."[10] To this day, governmental corruption remains a fact of business life in Nicaragua.

The political history of Nicaragua is a history of the rivalry between the two centers of economic power and political influence which developed around the towns of Granada on Lake Nicaragua, and León on Lake Managua. This rivalry has also influenced the evolution of the groups. Both towns were founded in 1524; the founders of Granada were said to have been the noblemen and leaders of the original exploration, while those of León were the more humble Spanish foot soldiers. The natural rivalry of these two cities combined with incidents involving religious differences, governmental corruption, and political betrayal resulted in an animosity between these two areas which was present before the close of the sixteenth century and which by the time of independence in 1821 had grown deep and bitter.[11] It made any agreement on the area's future following independence impossible and led to the political chaos captured in the following description:

> During this period, every town in Nicaragua seemed to have
> its own political disposition, independent army, and local
> candidate for presidential office. Anarchy reigned. On one
> occasion, while Granada and León were engaged in the bitter
> struggle for political dominance, an independent army from
> El Viejo attacked León. On another occasion in 1832, Ma-
> nagua, Masaya, and Matagalpa joined forces against the
> Central American Federation which momentarily had the sup-
> port of both León and Granada. Scarcely a year passed with-
> out two or three revolutions. Finally, on April 30, 1838,
> Nicaragua officially withdrew from the Central American
> Federation.[12]

It resulted in repeated civil wars between the Conservatives of Granada and the Liberals of León, one of which led the Liberals in the 1850s to invite an American, William Walker, and other "filibusters" to colonize Nicaragua. Walker arrived in 1855. He not only defeated the Conservatives and occupied Granada, but had himself elected President of the Republic, much to the chagrin of his original hosts. [13]

The rivalry led to dictatorships and revolts against these dictatorships which served as the pretext or stimulus for the direct intervention of the United States Marines in Nicaraguan affairs in 1909, 1912, and 1925. [14] The interventions, in turn, led to the guerrilla activities of César Augusto Sandino against the Americans from 1925 until 1933. [15]

The economic cost of this political chaos was very high. In addition to the men and materials wasted in war, agricultural activities were abandoned and between 1845 and 1945 much of the necessary construction of both a social and physical infrastructure was severely restricted. The chaos also paved the way for the emergence in 1936 of General Anastasio Somoza as Nicaragua's strong man and the founder of the special economic group which bears his name.

In modern Nicaragua, sectionalism is muted, due in part to the rise of Managua as the political and economic center, and in part to a ruling family dynasty of nearly 40 years. This family has carefully cultivated a national constituency, but the rivalry lives on under the surface, showing itself clearly in the shape of the business groups. The Banco de América Group is identified with the Conservatives of Granada, and the Banco Nicaraguense Group with the Liberals of León.

Economically, Nicaragua, like most underdeveloped countries, has always been and continues to be predominantly agricultural. Agricultural products and processed agricultural goods represent 80 percent of Nicaragua's production and virtually all of its exports; [16] agricultural exports are the single most important determinant of economic prosperity.

Nicaragua began exporting agricultural products to Panamá and Perú in the sixteenth century. Soon cattle, mules, and horses were being shipped north and south, while hides and tallow went to Europe. [17]

With the introduction of commercial coffee in the mid-1800s, Nicaragua's current economic dependence on agricultural exports took shape. Coffee was soon Nicaragua's primary cash crop. It contributed to the rise of Managua as the primary city of Nicaragua, attracted European immigrants, and remained, in spite of political turbulence, rising and falling world prices, and volcanic eruptions, Nicaragua's principal cash crop until 1950. [18]

Since 1950, cotton—like a second-booster rocket—has propelled the economy to an annual growth rate which during the last 14 years averaged 7 percent. While cotton is the principal engine of Nicaragua's recent economic expansion, the industrial sector has shown the greatest growth—an average of 9.9 percent per year between 1960 and 1974. [19] As Table B.2 shows, by 1970, the industrial sector represented a larger share of the gross national product than did agriculture, a deceptive statistic, however, since most of Nicaragua's industry is food processing and the processing of other agricultural products. [20]

Industrial growth has been stimulated by the expansion in cotton, as for example, in the start of textile and cotton oil industries, but also

TABLE B. 2

Structure of Nicaragua's Gross National Product, 1960, 1970, 1974
(millions of córdobas)

	1960	1970	1974
Total GNP in current prices	2, 348. 4	5, 858. 8	10, 551. 5
Total GNP in 1958 córdobas	2, 392. 6	4, 807. 6	6, 085. 5
Composition of GNP (percent of GNP at constant prices)			
Primary activities	24. 6	23. 7	23. 7
Agriculture	16. 2	15. 5	16. 5
Other	8. 4	8. 2	7. 2
Secondary activities	19. 0	26. 2	28. 0
Industry, manufacturing	15. 6	22. 3	22. 9
Construction	2. 2	3. 3	4. 4
Mining	1. 2	. 7	. 7
Tertiary activities	56. 4	50. 1	48. 3
Commerce	22. 4	21. 4	22. 7
Financial institutions	1. 5	2. 6	3. 1
Government, general			
transportation, communication, utilities, housing	6. 6	5. 1	4. 2
Other	25. 9	21. 0	18. 3
Imports as percent of GNP at current prices	25. 1	27. 1	40. 8
Exports as percent of GNP at current prices	22. 5	24. 8	28. 3

Note: The córdoba has maintained a 7:1 relation to the U.S. dollar throughout this period.
Source: Indicadores Económicos, Dept. de Estudios Económicos, Banco Central de Nicaragua 1, no. 2 (July 1975).

115

by the formation of the Central American Common Market in the early
1960s. [21] The Common Market has not been without its costs, but trade
among the Central American countries has risen dramatically and accounts in part for the notable increase in the percentage of external trade
to GNP from 1960 through 1974 shown in Tables B. 2 and B. 3.

The groups, as Chapter 3 makes clear, are most active in finance,
construction, and industry. An examination of the statistics in Table B.2
shows these sectors to have grown most rapidly in the last fifteen years.
During this period, both construction and finance have doubled their
percentage of gross national product.

Nicaragua's growth rate from 1950 to 1975, as Table B. 1 reveals,
has been attractive. During the first half of the 1960s GNP grew at an
average of 10. 1 percent per year. The fragility of this growth, however,
was demonstrated anew between 1965 and 1970; with the pause or end
of the cotton boom, the average growth rate dropped to 4. 4 percent. [22]

Since 1970 however, Nicaragua has enjoyed a growth rate of roughly
6. 1 percent in spite of the loss in production caused by the earthquake
of 1972. The causes of this boom have been high agricultural prices in
cattle, cotton, and coffee, and also the construction boom which followed the earthquake which destroyed the capital city Managua.

TABLE B. 3

Relative Importance of Nicaragua's Trading Partners, 1960-74
(percent of imports and exports)

	1960	1970	1974
Imports			
United States	53	36	32
Japan	7	6	7
Europe	14	14	17
Central America	4	25	23
Other	22	29	21
Exports			
United States	43	31	19
Japan	14	14	9
Central America	4	26	24
Europe	25	17	17
Other	14	12	21

Source: Indicadores Económicos, Cuadro 44, 1, no. 12 (July 1975),
Dept. de Estudios Económicos, Banco Central de Nicaragua.

A juxtaposition of Nicaragua's history and that of the groups shows that the groups have participated actively in the comparatively great prosperity of 1950 to 1975. They have been the leaders in some of the fastest-growing sectors in the economy. Their real strength, however, does not seem to be in the largest sector, agriculture, which apparently determines the rate of economic development of the country; rather their stronghold is in the smaller sectors of finance and industry.

NOTES

1. The description and history of Nicaragua in this study is not original, and it is not even based on an exhaustive study of the literature. The principal works used, those which able Nicaraguan historians have recommended to me as among the best available, are listed below: Pedro Belli, "An Inquiry Concerning the Growth of Cotton Farming in Nicaragua" (Ph. D. diss., University of California, Berkeley, 1968), for a description of the economic history of Nicaragua in the twentieth century; Neil Macaulay, The Sandino Affair (Chicago: Quadrangle Books, 1967), for a description of Nicaraguan history during the period of U. S. intervention in the first 35 years of the twentieth century; David R. Radell, Historical Geography of Western Nicaragua: The Spheres of Influence of León, Granada and Managua, 1519-1965. Report on Field Work carried out under ONR Contract Nonr-3656 (03), Project NR 388 067 (Department of Geography, University of California, Berkeley, James J. Parsons, Principal Investigator, 1969), for a geographical description to Nicaragua and summary of early history of Nicaragua; John Morris Ryan et al., Area Handbook for Nicaragua, DA Pam 550-88 (Washington, D. C.: U. S. Government Printing Office, 1970), for statistical information and general description; Sofonias Salvatierra, Contribución a la Historia de Centroamérica (Managua: Tiografía Progreso, 1939).

2. Ryan et al., op. cit., pp. 7, 8, 52, 55. The official results of the 1971 census reported in Table 3.1 shows Nicaragua's population at 1,974,900. It is the opinion of Dr. Gustavo Parajón, who has directed several medical teams working in rural areas, that this estimate is low. A recent vaccination campaign indicated that there were probably 300,000 more children in Nicaragua than the official census estimates.

3. Ibid., pp. 113-20.

4. International Bank for Reconstruction and Development, The Economic Development of Nicaragua (Baltimore: John Hopkins Press, 1953).

5. Ryan et al., op. cit., pp. 52, 61-74.

6. Radell, op. cit., pp. 50-64.

7. Ibid., p. 58.

8. Incredible as it seems, David R. Radell's detailed study of the slave trade supports the contemporary accounts which report that in the period from 1526 to 1548, 450, 000 to 600, 000 Indians were shipped as slaves from Nicaragua to Perú and Panamá and that so great was the slave trade, disease and war, that the native population of western Nicaragua was reduced "from more than a million to less than ten thousand within a period of sixty years." Ibid., pp. 66-80; the quoted passage is on p. 80.

9. Ibid., pp. 82, 84.

10. Ibid., pp. 107-22.

11. Ryan et al., op. cit., pp. 40-42.

12. Radell, op. cit., pp. 178-79.

13. Ryan et al., op. cit., pp. 44; Radell, op. cit., pp. 179-81. For a fascinating picture of Walker and his activities, see William Walker, The War in Nicaragua (1860; reprint ed., Detroit: Blaine Ethridge Books, 1971).

14. Macaulay, op. cit., pp. 23, 24.

15. Ibid.; Ryan et al., op. cit., pp. 45, 46.

16. Central Bank of Nicaragua, Informe Anual, 1970. The 80 percent figure was arrived at by adding the figure for agricultural and primary activities to that for industries which process agricultural products, and dividing the result by the figure for all primary and secondary activities.

17. Radell, op. cit., pp. 156-58.

18. Ibid., pp. 183-226.

19. In crop year 1948-49, the exports of cotton only came to 2, 200 metric tons. During the period from 1955 to 1966 these exports averaged 56, 850 metric tons per year, reaching over 100, 000 metric tons in 1965 and 1966. The increase in cotton exports was not at the expense of other traditional exports. Cotton-related industries, such as textiles and vegetable oils, were also stimulated by the growth in cotton production. Belli, op. cit., p. 60.

20. Department of Economic Studies, Banco Central de Nicaragua, Gross National Product, Revised Series, Preliminary Statistics, May 17, 1971.

21. Ernesto Cruz, Derecho, Desarrollo & Integración Regional en Centroamérica (San Salvador: Organización de Estados Centroamericanos, 1967), pp. 15-19.

22. Belli, op. cit., p. 25.

TABLE C. 1

Ranking of Potential Advantages of Group Membership by INCAE
M. B. A. Students and PAG Participants*

	Average Ranking		Evaluation (in percent)		
			Important Advantage	Advantage	No Advantage
Preferential access to credit	(1)	1. 8	89	8	3
Opportunities to invest	(2)	3. 5	58	40	3
Business from other members	(3)	4. 6	53	34	13
Social and psychological benefits	(9)	7. 4	8	61	32
Mutual support, administrative and technical	(6)	5. 3	18	71	11
Good treatment from the government	(4)	5. 0	40	47	13
Control of markets and prices	(5)	5. 2	42	42	16
Preferential treatment by other firms not of group	(7)	5. 4	24	63	13
Joint venture and other commercial relations with foreigners	(8)	6. 6	26	55	18

*Master in Business Administration students and Participants of
the Advanced Management Course at Instituto Centroamericano de
Administración de Empresas (INCAE), Managua, Nicaragua, 1971.
Source: Compiled by the author.

TABLE C. 2

Ranking of Potential Advantages by Subsamples[a]

	B.A. (9)	B.N. (10)	Other (11)	Participants (9)	Students (30)
Preferential access to credit (source of financing)	(1) 2.1	(1) 2.1	(2) 1.7	(1) 2.5	(1) 1.6
Opportunities for investment (vehicle for investment of funds)	(4) 3.4	(2) 3.0	(1) 1.7	(3) 3.2	(2) 3.5
Business from other group members (same)	(3) 3.2	(3) 3.2	(3) 4.9	(2) 2.6	(4) 5.1
Social and psychological benefits (same)	(2) 2.6	(4) 4.0	(7) 5.4	(8) 7.6	(9) 7.0
Mutual support administratively and technically (same)	(7) 5.9	(8) 5.9	(5) 5.2	(5) 5.1	(6) 5.1
Good treatment from the government (political benefits)	(8) 6.4	(7) 5.5	(8) 5.8	(7) 6.0	(3) 4.7
Control of markets (same)	(6) average 5.4[b]			(6) 5.4	(7) 5.5
Joint venture and other commercial relations with foreigner (business relations with foreigner and foreign investments)	(5) 5.3	(5) 5.0	(4) 4.9	(9) 7.8	(8) 6.7

[a]Nomenclature in parentheses is that used in interview list.
[b]Only five responded due to late insertion in the list.
Source: Compiled by the author.

TABLE C. 3

Preference in Quantity of Credit to Group Firms

Question: All the companies (four) come to the financial institutions of the group to ask for a long-term loan for expansion. . . . If to Company C they would give a normal amount of credit, how much would they give to the other firms?

	Answers (34) by Percent					
	Much More	More	Same	Less	Much Less	Summary Index*
To Company A (a firm of same group)	59	29	12	—	—	1.47
To Company B (a firm of other group)	—	9	28	34	28	-.81
To Company C (a national firm unaffiliated to any group)			Standard of Comparison			0
To Company D (a foreign firm or subsidiary)	—	19	56	22	3	-.09

*Weighted average on scale of 2.00 to -2.00.
Source: Compiled by the author.

TABLE C. 4

Preference in Interest Rates to Group Firms

Question: If the real or effective interest rate on the loan given to Company C is normal, what would be the interest rate for the others?

	Answers (34) by Percent					
	Much Lower	Lower	Same	Higher	Much Higher	Summary Index*
Company A (firm of own group)	6	21	73	—	—	.33
Company B (firm of other group)	—	—	78	3	19	-.41
Company C (a national firm unaffiliated to any group)			Standard of Comparison			0
Company D (foreign subsidiary)	—	7	93	—	—	.07

*Weighted Average on scale of 2.00 to -2.00.
Source: Compiled by the author.

TABLE C. 5

Preference in Quantity of Credit to Group Persons

Question: Each man asks for a loan from the Bank for his own
business or personal affairs. It is probable that if the financial
institutions are willing to give Mr. C. a loan for a standard
amount, they would probably give the others:

	Answers (34) by Percent					
	Much More	More	Same	Less	Much Less	Index
Mr. A (member of that group)	63	30	7	—	—	1.56
Mr. B (member of the other group)	—	46	32	4	11	.20
Mr. C (a national figure without affiliation)			Standard			0
Mr. D (foreigner)	—	7	63	26	4	.27

Note: The comments accompanying the replies to these situations
throw some light on the way credit allocation is affected by group relations.

First, several answers emphasized that the main criterion for a
loan was not whether the firm was a member of the group, but whether
it had guarantees, a solid business, and so forth. The preference only
applies to those situations in which the loan applicants have already
been screened through these multiple filters and in all other respects
except group affiliation are the same.

Second, the case of a firm from one group even approaching the
bank of the other group for a loan seemed to most highly unusual. Seven
indicated that the firm would never ask for a loan from the other group's
firms, and five felt that if it did ask, it would get nothing. (Several
assumed that if the other group's firm was coming to the bank, it was
because the firm was somewhat independent. In this case, the bank
might treat it the same or even show a slight preference in the hopes of
wooing it away from the other group.)

Third, the only noticeable difference between the case of a group
firm and a group-affiliated person was the treatment afforded persons in
the other groups. While another group's firm will probably meet adverse
discrimination (Index -. 81 from Table C. 3), a member of the other group
might well receive preferential treatment (Index . 20 from Table C. 5). The
member of the other group will receive credit, perhaps even more than
usual, in an attempt to woo him, especially if he is a somewhat marginal
or not fully committed member of the group. He will also be treated differ-
entially in his personal request because "reciprocity" can than be expected
in the future. These replies helped explain an interesting fact I discovered
early in the study. Many of the group members who were clearly identified
with one of the groups were borrowers of or did some business with the
financial institutions of the other group. Many evidently feel the need for
personal insurance and do not want to depend on any one group or person
exclusively.

Fourth, preference is likely to be in amounts of credit or in the terms
of credit, but not in lower interest rates. This is because interest rates
charged by the banks are fixed by government regulation and are generally
lower than what a true market rate would be.

Source: Compiled by the author.

TABLE C.6

Nicaragua: Food Processing and Beverage Industries;
Selected Financial Data, by Group and Nongroup Firms, 1968

	11 Group Firms	14 Nongroup Firms
Average size (millions of córdobas)		
Net profits*	2.64	.75
Net sales	23.50	11.20
Net worth	14.80	4.40
Assets	25.90	8.40
Liquidity		
Acid test	.72	.62
Current ratio	1.87	1.28
Use of Debt		
Total Debt/Total assets (percent)	43.00	47.50
Interest paid/Total debt (percent)	6.21	8.42
Trading on equity (leverage)	1.37	1.24
Profitability (percent)		
Net Profits*/Equity	16.39	16.32
Profits before interest/Total assets	12.10	13.21

*Before income taxes.
Note: The nongroup sample does not include 12 government and smaller non-group firms which were included in the larger sample in the source. The weaknesses and origins of the underlying data are discussed in the source, pp. 28-29.
Source: Prepared from the heterogeneous sample in Professor José Nicolás Marín's unpublished doctoral thesis for the Harvard Business School, 1971, "Industrial Finance in Nicaragua," Exhibit V-5, p. 108.

TABLE C.7

Investment Opportunities of Group Members

Question: In this section, we try to identify the advantages to the businessman in being part of the group. In order to make a comparison specific, we will . . . talk of four persons. All are wealthy men with businesses or properties. All have a high social status. Mr. A is a typical member of your group; Mr. B is a typical member of the other group; Mr. C is not a member of any group; and Mr. D is a foreigner not a member of any group . . .
For a wealthy man, the opportunities to place his savings in attractive investments is important. If the typical Mr. C has a normal number of opportunities to make investments in Central America during the course of a year, it is probable that the number of attractive investments which are offered to the others would be: (much greater, greater, the same, fewer, much fewer).

	Answers (32) by Percent					
	Much Greater	Greater	Same	Fewer	Much Fewer	Summary Index
Mr. C (national)			Standard			0
Mr. A & B (group members)	56	40	4	--	--	1.52
Mr. D (foreign businessman)	3	19	48	26	3	0.07

*Weighted average on a scale of 2.00 to −2.00.
Source: Compiled by the author.

TABLE C. 8

Profitability of Investment Opportunities of Group Members

Question: If the opportunities of investment of Mr. C are considered of normal profitability, the opportunities of investment of the others will probably be: (much more profitable, more profitable, same, less profitable, much less profitable).

	Answers (27) by Percent					Summary Index*
	Much More Profitable	More Profitable	Same	Less Profitable	Much Less Profitable	
Mr. C (unaffiliated national)		Standard				0
Mr. A and B (of the groups)	22	56	22	—	—	1.00
Mr. D (foreigner)	—	32	48	20	—	.12

*Weighted average on scale of 2.00 to -2.00.
Source: Compiled by the author.

TABLE C. 9

Evaluation of Investment Opportunities of Group Members in Relation to Respondent's Affiliation

Question: What are the investment opportunities of group members in comparison with average Nicaraguan businessmen?

	Answers (32) by Percent					Summary Index*
Respondent's Affiliation	Much More	More	Same	Fewer	Much Fewer	
B.A. (9)	33	67	—	—	—	1. 33
B.N. (12)	42	46	12	—	—	1. 30
Other (11)	91	9	—	—	—	1. 91

*Weighted average on scale of 2.00 to -2.00.
Source: Compiled by the author.

TABLE C.10

Obligation of Intragroup Business

Question: Imagine that you are about to purchase an automobile (or some other thing). Do you feel an obligation to purchase it from X, who is a member of your group? In other words, do you feel that one of the obligations of being in the group is to give fellow group members your business?

Response	Answers (19) by Percent
Yes, even at personal disadvantage	(3) 16
Yes, preference but not at disadvantage	(13) 68
No obligation	(3) 15

Note: Two respondents commented that they would probably get special discounts if they bought from a fellow group member; three of those who preferred to deal with a fellow group member, but not at a disadvantage, said that they would hold open bidding.

Source: Compiled by the author.

TABLE C.11

Government Treatment

Question: Four firms of the same size have to deal with the government in various ways. If the effort and cost for Company C, which is a national firm unaffiliated with any group or the ruling family, is considered normal, what would be the effort and cost for each of the other firms affiliated with the Banco de América Group, affiliated with the Banco Nicaraguense Group, and a foreign subsidiary to secure a) licenses of import or export, b) secure permission to operate or for construction, c) secure favorable tax classification, d) secure loans from governmental institutions, e) secure tariff barriers, f) defend itself from discrimination by some particular agency or person in the government?

	Answers (33) by Percent				
	Much Less Effort and Cost	Less Cost	Same Cost	More Cost	Much More Cost	Index*
National firms			Standard			0
Group firms (overall)	17.2	37.4	41.7	3.7	—	.68
Foreign firms	4.0	28.0	60.0	5.0	3.0	.25

*Weighted average of replies on scale of 2.00 to -2.00.
Source: Compiled by the author.

125

TABLE C. 12

Cost and Effort in Securing Same Treatment as Unaffiliated National Firm

	Summary Indexes*		
	Group	Foreign	National
Average overall ranking	.68	.25	0
Individual ranking			
Import and export licenses	.55	.12	0
Permission to operate or build	.65	.16	0
Appropriate tax classification	.52	.30	0
Loans for governmental institutions	.65	.33	0
Tariff barriers	.53	.38	0
Defense against discrimination	1.09	.38	0
Government contracts	.81	.05	0

*Weighted average of replies on the following scale:

2.00	1.00	0	-1.00	-2.00
Much Less	Less	Same	More	Much More

Source: Compiled by the author.

TABLE C. 13

Treatment by Independent Suppliers

Question: Now imagine that these four companies all in the same industry, all of roughly the same size, purchase materials from a firm we will call Supplier X. Supplier X does not belong to any group or have special ties with any of the firms. If he wants to, there are a lot of ways Supplier X can treat one firm more favorably than another—for example, by lower prices, better terms of credit, and preference during periods of scarcity. In comparison with the treatment which Supplier X normally gives to Firm C, the national firm, how would he on the average treat a group firm? How would he treat a foreign firm?

	Answers (34) by Percent					
	Much Better	Better	Same	Worse	Much Worse	Summary Index*
National nongroup firms	Standard of Comparison					0
Group firms	6	47	47	—	—	.59
Foreign firms	—	6	91	—	—	.03
Additional comments:						
This is important advantage	2	—	—	—	—	
Only small advantage, if any	1	1	—	—	—	
Managers' personnel relations						
much more important	1	1	—	—	—	
Preference in conditions not prices	2	—	—	—	—	
Preference even in prices	1	—	—	—	—	
Supplier considers group more solid	1	—	—	—	—	
Supplier thinking of help he can						
get in future from group	1	2	—	—	—	
Supplier thinking of large volume						
whole group represents	1	—	—	—	—	

*Weighted average of replies on scale of 2.00 to -2.00.
Note: A decisive majority of the interviewees regarded the following two statements as false:
● Because I am a member of the group, suppliers and sellers of equipment give me more favorable terms than other similar firms.
● It is easier for me to get good employees than for other similar businesses, although I pay the same salaries, because working with a group is popular.
Source: Compiled by the author.

TABLE C. 14

Help in Time of Need

Question: Assume that one of the long standing members of the group who is not one of your relatives or intimate personal friends comes upon hard times in his business. He needs financing, but the financial institutions of the group, because of the high standards of stewardship imposed on them in handling the public's money, don't feel that they can lend him the money. Would you feel any obligation to help him, even to the extent of lending him money?

Responses	Answers (18)
Obligation to help at personal risk	0
Obligation at no personal risk	15
No obligation	3

Note: What interpretation should be given to the reluctance to take personal risks for a fellow group member? Two interpretations are possible. One is that when in the hypothetical case it says that the financial institutions won't bail him out, the implication is that the financial institutions consider the situation hopeless. If the institutions have decided to abandon X, then the group has decided to abandon him. If personal reasons of family or friendship are absent, most interviewees will wonder why they should not do the same and so will answer that they have no obligation. Supporting this is the comment of an interviewee in another context who stated that "Groups will not let one of their businesses die."

There is another interpretation, however, which I find more persuasive. The fact that the bank cannot or will not lend the member money is evidence that the situation is serious, but not that the group has decided to abandon him. The group association as a group is primarily "to make money." Friends and relatives are for help in time of need. Members of the group feel an obligation to show concern, to help analyze the problem and, if possible, to solve it. This help is not likely to be free. Unless his difficulties are in no sense his own fault—the result, for example, of some dramatic act of God—the member will probably lose control of his business and a good portion of the equity. With the loss of his economic power, he will probably become a marginal member of the group. This interpretation reinforces the economic nature of the group and raises doubts as to the strength of group loyalty, trust, and confidence, in the absence of family or intimate ties of friendship.

Source: Compiled by the author.

TABLE C. 15

Social and Psychological Benefits of Group Membership

Question: To be a member of a group also has its social and psychological advantages.

	Answers (33) by Percent				
	Extremely Important Advantage	Clear Advantage	Little Advantage	No Advantage	Summary Index*
Friendship and social contact with other intelligent and successful businessmen	36	36	24	3	2.04
The feeling of being involved in a business activity of considerable significance	23	52	16	10	1.89
Intellectual stimulation and exposure to exciting ideas and new business techniques	19	35	29	16	1.56
The respect of the business community and a position of leadership therein	34	44	13	9	2.03

*Weighted average on a scale of 3.00 to 0
Source: Compiled by the author.

APPENDIX D:
THE BIRTH OF THE
BANCO NICARAGUENSE GROUP

The following description of the birth of the Banco Nicaraguense Group by Dr. Eduardo Montealegre, taken from my interview notes of January 17, 1971, is included here as an appendix because it presents not only a vivid picture of one of two groups studied, but expresses a number of the salient characteristics and policies of business groups in the language of a group leader.

The development of the group (Banco Nicaraguense) was not a conscious activity, planned from the start, but something which gradually developed . . . .

In approximately 1952, I returned to Nicaragua with some experience in banking in Guatemala and in Washington with the IMF. I had the idea at that time of developing a bank which might also provide other intermediary services, like those of a savings and loan bank. At the time, I had ideas and experience but no capital.

My initial concern was to find supporters with capital, business connections, governmental influence, and sufficient position in the community to create the goodwill and confidence necessary to ensure the bank's success. The first person I approached was a friend of my family, a lawyer, who was quite an entrepreneur, Dr. Salvador Guerrero Montalbán. He agreed that the idea was a good one. Together, we contacted a select group of people to join us in the venture. All were men of business, although we also included several men in the government, but from different parts of the country, León, Managua, Diriamba, etc. These men were all approached individually, but the final planning session was held with everyone together in one of the hotels. In that meeting, we put forth the plan which called for the raising of C$3,000,000 [córdobas] in capital. Half of the capital was to be sold to the assembled men and the other half was to be sold in small blocs to businessmen whom we hoped would become customers of the bank. No one person was to buy more than 10 percent of the outstanding stock.

A major hurdle was getting government permission to open a bank, a project accomplished by convincing General Somoza (the father) that the time had come for this sort of institution in Nicaragua's development. Somoza also subscribed to a group members' bloc of stock in the bank. The final group of owners included people who had been in the

business of lending money before, and several foreigners
resident in the country who had some appreciation of sophisticated finance.

I resigned my position in the United States to become
general manager of the Bank in January. By March or April,
the Bank was opened. By the end of the year, we had made
a profit and paid shareholders 10 percent dividend. The
Bank expanded rapidly . . . .

Within two years, I believe, the savings and loan operation was begun as a separate institution for legal reasons.
First, we found a dynamic, young manager to head the operation. Then, in preparing the capital subscription, we
eliminated several of the bank's original subscribers and
added several other people, especially those with construction business contacts. Shortly thereafter, the Savings and
Loan Bank founded a construction company, although later
the stock of the construction company was issued as a stock
dividend to shareholders of the Savings and Loan Association.

Later, the Bank and several of its shareholders purchased
30 percent of the stock of La Protectora, an insurance company, but we did not take over management until five years
ago, when earnings were down to only C$16,000. At that
time, the directorate was changed, the manager replaced and
the firm reorganized. Earnings grew to a level of C$2,000,000
this past year.

The group's next move was into an investment banking
operation, INDESA, in 1966. About this time, the group began to think of itself more as a group, and we began to take
steps to organize ourselves as such. The bank took out the
ownership interest in the financiera. We had wanted the
bank to own over 50 percent of the stock but laws only allowed us to own 25 percent, so we had to ensure bank control by clauses in the stock which gave us a right of veto
over board of directors' decisions and other personal decisions. . . .

ABOUT THE AUTHOR

HARRY W. STRACHAN is Associate Professor of Finance and International Business, and Director of the Development Banking Program at the Instituto Centroamericano de Administración de Empresas (INCAE) in Nicaragua, Central America. Dr. Strachan received his B. A. Degree from Wheaton College, Wheaton, Illinois, a J. D. from the Harvard Law School, and a D. B. A. from the Harvard Business School.

For the last six years Dr. Strachan has worked in Central America, where he was born. His work has included considerable consultation with organizations in the private and public sectors, writing and supervision of over 50 teaching cases and notes in the area of finance, and the design and teaching of numerous M.B.A. and Executive courses in Central America, Panamá, the Dominican Republic, Colombia, Ecuador, Bolivia, and Brazil.

ECONOMIC NATIONALISM IN LATIN AMERICA
Shoshana Baron Tancer

INCOME DISTRIBUTION POLICIES AND ECONOMIC
GROWTH IN SEMI-INDUSTRIALIZED COUNTRIES: A
Comparative Analysis of Iran, Mexico, Brazil, and
South Korea
Robert E. Looney

THE NATION-STATE AND TRANSNATIONAL CORPO-
RATION IN CONFLICT: With Special Reference to
Latin America
edited by Jon P. Gunnemann

MERCHANTS AS PROMOTERS OF RURAL DEVELOPMENT:
An Indian Case Study
Paul A. London

THE PUBLIC ADMINISTRATION OF ECONOMIC DEVEL-
OPMENT
Irving Swerdlow